Indentured is wonderful, perfectly timed and written with an extraordinary innocence and honesty. Atul Gupta will absolutely hate this book, which is why South Africans should buy it in their tens of thousands. It confirms, if confirmation were needed, the extent of the Gupta family's contempt for South Africans and our country, and their contempt for the many Indian professionals hired with false promises to assist with the launch of their television channel ANN7.

Jacob Zuma will also hate this book. He has always tried to obfuscate the extent of his ties to the Gupta family, arguing that they merely employ his son. Not so. Indentured *reveals for the first time Zuma's close and personal involvement – and the lengths he went to in order to try to hide it – with the launch of ANN7. It is the perfect full stop, in a way, to the leaks of the Gupta emails which so dominated the news in 2017.*

It confirms, time and again, because the author is a real person and not an anonymous Twitter account, that the Guptas, perhaps particularly the obsequious and bullying brother, Atul, care nothing for South Africans.

On more than one occasion the author reveals not only that the Guptas boasted to fellow Indians how they had the South African government in their pockets but also that even when Zuma leaves office, they will own his successor. This glorious little book helps make that, thankfully, less likely. I cannot recommend it more highly.

– Peter Bruce

Indentured

Indentured
Behind the Scenes at Gupta TV

Rajesh Sundaram

Note to the reader

The events described in this book took place as remembered by Rajesh Sundaram. We've tried to verify whether the meetings and conversations took place as described in the book. Former president Jacob Zuma was approached for corroboration, as were brothers Atul and Ajay Gupta. To date we have received no responses from them, and they may well have a different interpretation of events, and by pointing this out we leave it to you, dear reader, to make up your mind.

First published by Jacana Media (Pty) Ltd in 2018

10 Orange Street
Sunnyside
Auckland Park 2092
South Africa
+2711 628 3200
www.jacana.co.za

© Rajesh Sundaram, 2018

All rights reserved.

ISBN 978-1-4314-0992-1

Cover design by publicide
Set in Stempel Garamond 11/16.5pt
Printed and bound by ABC Press, Cape Town
Job no. 003047

See a complete list of Jacana titles at www.jacana.co.za

I would like to dedicate this book to my late father KC Sundaram and my mother Geeta Sundaram. I am what I am today because of them.

Prologue

30 August 2013

THE SCENE WAS STRAIGHT out of a low-budget Bollywood potboiler. And it must have been rehearsed in much the same way, as how it unfolded showed that the two main players would have discussed, planned and gone over it many times before I was summoned into the mezzanine-floor director's office. It was an office that Laxmi Goel, small-time Indian real estate company owner and director of Essel Media, used when he was in Midrand.

Atul Gupta and Laxmi were waiting for me. They are two of the trinity of stakeholders who owned Infinity Media; 35 per cent each. The remaining 30 per cent was owned by a sleeping partner. Infinity Media was the primary controller of the 24-hour news channel African News Network 7 (ANN7).

Both were dressed low-budget Bollywood style as well. Atul, spilling out of his blue suit, sat with his legs crossed, his red silk tie meandering over the crisp white shirt that stretched over the ample bulge of his protruding belly. Laxmi was dressed in a brown suit and at his throat he sported a burnt orange pocket scarf. The two sat together on a two-seater couch; there was no one else in the large room.

As I opened the door and walked in, Laxmi gestured for me to sit down on the couch opposite them. There was a large coffee table between the couches, all part of the cheap knock-down office furniture imported from China in huge containers and assembled by Indian labourers overnight in Midrand. Atul and Laxmi were both businessmen who believed in saving the pennies.

At the other end of the room was a large office table behind which was Laxmi's chair. It was a large chair, considering that he was not a very tall man. Across the table were three smaller chairs for visitors. Usually, he sat on his chair looking for all the world like a deity in a temple, with his visitors looking like seekers of enlightenment sitting on theirs. The table was bare as it was not used much. There was no computer nor were there any other office accessories on it. Laxmi was based in India and only came to South Africa for a few days every now and then.

The couches were reserved for special guests. Laxmi sat there to drink black tea with people he wanted to entertain.

'What have you planned?' he asked in a loud, harsh tone.

In the four months since I first met him to discuss taking on the position of editor of ANN7, Laxmi had always spoken to me politely and softly. He spoke in a rural north Indian Hindi dialect. He was never comfortable speaking English. But now I felt like a prisoner standing in front of a kangaroo court and waiting for the firing squad. I had handed in my resignation papers three days earlier, disgusted with the lack of editorial integrity, abuse and surveillance of staff and my inability to convince management to improve working conditions for the journalists at ANN7. The two had not taken kindly to it and were angry that I had subsequently turned down unconvincing offers to stay on.

As I walked into the room, I couldn't help but realise that there were more than the usual number of armed bodyguards in the office.

I decided I would not get provoked; that I would be respectful but firm about my decision. I had to ignore the insults and move out of this organisation with dignity.

'Sir, you know my decision already. I have resigned and I have already said I would like to be relieved as soon as possible. I am sure the company will pay me what it owes me for overtime.'

'So you don't want to take a small break and come back and re-join us? Don't want to think about it?' Laxmi asked me in Hindi.

I knew instantly that they were playing mind games with me. I had got to know the two well enough over the past three months to realise that. I decided to stay focused and not be drawn into this trick.

'You know, sir, the way things are managed here is not what was promised to me. Things need to change if you want me to reconsider my decision. Taking a break and getting back into the same mess is not what I want to do…'

Atul was glaring at me while I was speaking to Laxmi. His anger spilled over and he couldn't contain himself. Butting into the conversation, he interjected, 'But Mr Goel, he has already resigned. He has already told everyone, he has told HR, Aslam and others.' Aslam Kamal was the creative head at the Gupta-owned *The New Age* newspaper. 'If we ask him to stay it will be seen as – he showed us the middle finger and we are begging him to stay. He should beg *us*. What is he…? What…? Just an editor.

'And what is this final settlement you are seeking from Nazeem?' he asked, turning to me. Nazeem Howa was ANN7's group chief executive officer. 'If you quit we will not pay a cent more than your salary up until today… you are owed only five days' pay. And we will give you your return ticket to India only if you sign in the next hour. If you don't sign, you will get nothing. No ticket and no money. Take me to court. I have all the top lawyers in my pocket; let's see how much you will get.' He was seething with rage now.

I took a deep breath and tried to make sense of the game they were playing with me.

'Look Rajesh,' continued Laxmi. 'Do you really want to ruin your career by seeking more than what is due on your salary? You know how powerful I am in India. I make mountains out of molehills and molehills out of mountains in no time. You will not get any money here and you will never ever get a salary again. It is in your best interest to accept what we are giving you, take your ticket and get back to India. Anyway, I will see you when you are in Delhi.'

He said this in a threatening kind of way, looking at Atul for acknowledgement. It sounded to me as though he wanted me to understand that he would have my bones broken. This was getting too much for me. I was sitting in front of two billionaires who were trying to bully me into signing away what I considered my legitimate dues.

'Sir, I respect what you say, but I will not sign something I am not convinced about. There are courts and institutions in South Africa. I have a right to appeal what you are saying before them. If they say that my claims are untenable, I will respect that. I have a right to be heard in a court of law.'

'You are a bloody fool. You have no respect for the people who employ you,' Atul shot back. 'You are such a *Zaleel*,[1] you gave back the scarf I gave you and the 500 rand I paid the doctor through that lowly Malla.' Everyone knew the general handyman and Gupta

---

1   *Zaleel*: Meaning in Hindi/Urdu: A noxious or mischievous animal; especially, noxious little animals or insects

loyalist simply as Malla. 'How dare you? Is that how you repay my kindness, by returning things through servants? You are such a big man that you will not come to me and say thank you?'

I had had enough of Atul's arrogance. I had seen him speak in that tone with other people; the tone of a feudal lord.

Atul had given me the woollen scarf on 19 August 2013, the day President Jacob Zuma visited the ANN7 studio in Midrand, two days before the official launch of the channel.

I had been pulled out of an editorial meeting and told to be part of the reception committee. Although I had known that President Zuma would visit that morning, the exact time of his arrival was only conveyed at the last moment.

I was standing at the ANN7 studio gate with Atul, Laxmi and Nazeem, waiting for the presidential convoy to arrive. It was very cold that morning and the chilly winds made things worse. Because I had been hurriedly pulled out of the meeting I had not had time to grab my jacket.

I was shivering in the cold, and Atul gave me his woollen scarf to wrap around my neck. It was a very human gesture that seemed to indicate that beneath the harsh exterior was a kindly person.

After the meeting, I took it home with me, meaning to send it to the dry cleaners before returning it to him. In the meanwhile he sent me an SMS asking to return the scarf. I SMSed back saying it was at the dry cleaners and that I would return it to him at the earliest.

On 25 August, just four days after the launch, I was starting to take strain healthwise. The intense pressure, constant work, three months without a break and the long hours – as much as 16 to 18 hours a day – were unsustainable. I had had a blackout two

Indentured

weeks before; it was frightening but I recovered. However, on the 25th I again felt myself on the verge of blacking out. I was in the newsroom and felt weak with palpitations. I sat down and asked one of my colleagues to take me to hospital immediately. I blacked out for a few seconds as I put my head on a table nearby.

I was coping with an enormous amount of pressure at work. While understanding the attitude of the media, the unrelenting derision of the responses on social media to ANN7's miserable launch as well as the constant system failures and mistakes made by the poorly trained team were taking their toll on me.

My colleague went to arrange for a company car and at the same time informed Nazeem and Atul about my situation. They came downstairs almost immediately and volunteered to take me to the hospital in a car from Atul's fleet. I was feeling terribly unwell, but also very embarrassed by all the fuss I was creating in the newsroom.

Nazeem jumped into the back seat, and Atul sat next to his driver.

My colleague helped me into the back seat next to Nazeem and shut the door.

Atul took me to see a Dr Cassim who prescribed medication for high blood pressure and a sedative and recommended at least two days' rest. Atul generously handed over the 500 rand consultation fee before I could take out my wallet. He took the prescription and diagnosis note from Dr Cassim and put it in his pocket.

'I will take it from here,' I said. 'Just give me the prescription; I will buy the medicine, go home and rest.'

'No, you come home with me and stay at our guest house for the night.' I was taken aback by his uncharacteristic generosity.

At 8 am the next day, a car from the Gupta family fleet was waiting at the Gupta guest house to take me to the office. 'You must hurry up, sir; Mr Atul Gupta is waiting for you at office,' the driver instructed me.

The weeks between President Zuma's visit and the post-launch pressure were crazy. Earlier, on the day I was summoned to the director's room, I had collected the woollen scarf from the dry cleaners and stopped at the ATM to draw the cash to repay Atul.

I was greatly touched by his generosity – lending me his woollen scarf, then getting me to his doctor, sorting out the prescription and even going as far as to put me up in the guest house for the night, and I wanted to meet with him in person to return the scarf, repay the cash and express my thanks.

As I arrived at the office, I met Malla, who told me that Nazeem and Infinity Media human resources (HR) head Margriet Coetzee were waiting for me in one of the meeting rooms. I was asked to meet them immediately before attending the meeting with Atul and Laxmi.

'Can I come back in a few minutes? I have to give this to Mr Gupta,' I told Malla, pointing to the sealed plastic bag that held the dry-cleaned scarf.

'I am going to him right now; I can take it for you if you want.'

I agreed, somewhat reluctantly, and handed him the scarf and the money, explaining that it was for the doctor's appointment he had paid for me. Malla took the bag and money and I left to meet Nazeem and Margriet.

They tried convincing me to stay and I politely declined. I had taken a principled decision and there was no way I would reconsider.

'If you stay you get a hundred thousand rand a month, if you go you will get five days' pay. You should think about this,' Nazeem said.

'Five days' pay? What about the leave encashment and the overtime that I have worked?'

'You don't get that as per South African labour laws,' Margriet said with a smile.

'I am leaving anyway and I will check with an expert about what the laws say.'

Looking back, it's interesting for me to see the path my decision took me on. But it's a decision I will never regret.

～

When I heard Atul's outburst and abuse afterwards in the director's room about the scarf and money, it left me angry and full of regret about my decision to join ANN7.

It was an enormous undertaking I had embarked upon. After being so berated by him I felt great resentment and thought bitterly of how I had slogged to set up his television station. Was it worth it? I had really extended myself to try to pull it together, quite often working for up to 18 hours a day in the three months leading up to this point. And yet for all that, he saw me, and treated me, as nothing more than a servant.

He thought he was my master, treating me with contempt by using the derogatory term *Zaleel* for not personally thanking him with folded hands.

The tension in the room was broken by a knock on the door. It was Atul's assistant. She opened the door and looked in; with a gesture that had become unpleasantly familiar, Gupta motioned at her angrily to go. She left quickly and closed the door behind her. Then there was absolute silence for about two minutes.

'Look, you know what is good for you. Go back into the next room, sign the document and then go away. You do not want to see our bad side,' Laxmi shot at me in Hindi.

'Go out, sign, get out. I will see you Delhi,' he said in his broken English.

Although I was angry at the insults and humiliation they were piling on me, I decided I would not let them provoke me. I made up my mind to leave and wanted to carefully consider how I could challenge the settlement amount they had unilaterally decided upon.

'All right, sir, I will go now,' I said and walked towards the door.

I said I would go, but I had no intention of going to the next room and signing a document that I believed was unfair. I decided to walk out of the office and to my hotel room.

The newsroom and reception area were swarming with Gupta family bodyguards that day. There was one in an overcoat standing just outside the room. He was white, like most of the Gupta bodyguards, and tall. I had seen him around many times in the office compound and at the Gupta residence. I'd stopped being surprised by seeing them and had reached an easy level of familiarity.

All of the Gupta family bodyguards, who also double up as drivers, are armed at all times and are always connected with a hands-free wireless communication system. While some of them conceal their weapons behind an overcoat, others carry their guns openly strapped to their thighs.

As I walked away from the director's room towards the stairway that connected the mezzanine floor to the ground floor reception, I heard someone call my name.

It was a firm voice, not loud.

'Mr Sundaram, can you come this way please?'

It was the bodyguard I had just exchanged smiles with. I went up to him with growing unease.

'Can you please follow me, sir?' He took me to the small conference room next to the director's room and asked me to come in. This was the room Atul and Laxmi had asked me to go to. I was suspicious, but did as I was asked to do.

As I entered the room I saw a sheepish Margriet who moments before had tried to get me to sign a document forcing me to stay, with a familiar-looking piece of paper in her hand. The bodyguard shut the door behind me and stood with his arms crossed inside the room.

'Rajesh, can you please sign this now?' she asked.

'What is it, Margriet?' I asked, taking the piece of paper from her

Indentured

hand. 'But this is the same offer I said I will not sign. I cannot sign this. I will not,' I said.

Margriet looked at the bodyguard and he looked at me.

I smiled at him and said, 'I will not sign any document that I do not agree with. If there is a disagreement, Margriet, you are a lawyer. There are courts and recourse to arbitration.'

While the bodyguard and Margriet looked at each other, I opened the door and walked out into the area where the programming team sits.

The bodyguard followed me. 'Sir, can you please come back to the room.'

I knew what they were trying to do now. They wanted to intimidate me into signing the document. It was clear that the bodyguard was in the room with the specific purpose of strong-arming me. I ran down the stairs and made my way into the reception area. The bodyguard followed me. I crossed the reception area and went out through the main door. The bodyguard quickened his pace as soon as he was outside the building.

'Mr Sundaram, come back up. Mr Gupta wants to see you. You have not signed the document; I cannot allow you to go.'

I did not stop. 'Please tell Mr Gupta I do not want the settlement he is offering me. I do not want to meet him. I am going home now and will soon go back to India. I have quit; you cannot chase and intimidate me.'

I could see that Atul and Laxmi wanted me to sign a settlement immediately to ensure that I did not challenge it later in a court of law. They were wary of the bad press that would follow.

He followed me for the next few steps. I could hear him say something into his hands-free communication system. As I walked briskly down the driveway towards the main security gate, I saw him running back inside the building, probably to brief Atul about his little misadventure.

As I went through the main security gate, I could hear the guard's wireless set crackle. I could hear Malla's voice ask him if I had passed through the gate. He said yes.

I could sense trouble brewing. I was fully aware that the Guptas were powerful businessmen with seemingly little regard for the law. They had a feudal attitude and in my experience did not indulge any dissent. I felt that if they could go as far as intimidating and forcing their editor to sign a document he did not agree with, as they were clearly trying to do now, they would have no qualms getting him beaten up – or worse – if they thought they could get away with it.

I quickly got out of the Corporate Park complex in which the studio and newsroom are located and set off down the main road. My cellphone battery was dead, and it was getting dark. I felt vulnerable, exhausted and very threatened.

During my stay in Midrand, it hadn't been necessary, and nor had I had the time, to buy a car. I was therefore dependent on the transport provided by the office and had very little sense of the roads and directions.

I walked against the traffic, as I was sure they would send someone after me. They were determined to get me to sign the settlement document. Knowing Atul, he would do it by hook or by crook.

I had been staying with a friend until a few days before and had moved out of his house and into a hotel, as his wife and son had come to join him from India. I had asked him to keep my luggage until I made an alternate arrangement. One of the reasons I left his house was also my increasing differences with Atul and Laxmi. I was sure the position of anyone who maintained contact with me after I resigned would become very difficult. I had known Atul to be a very vindictive individual in his dealings with ex-employees, and so I knew I needed to keep my friend safe.

I was always welcome to go back to his house, but my current circumstances would scare his wife and son, and my presence would have got him into Atul and Laxmi's black book.

As I walked in the dark, I felt uneasy and tired. I had not slept the previous night. Every muscle in my body was aching.

The day before, as a precaution, I had asked another friend to keep my passport at his house. I feared for my safety after I resigned, especially in the event of a disagreement. If my passport fell into Gupta hands, I would be trapped.

I had moved into the Cotswold Inn at Blue Hills. I had arrived with just a few clothes and my wallet. The hotel was far away from Corporate Park, which I'd just left, and with the dead battery in my phone there was no way I could call a taxi. Added to that, the hotel had been booked through the ANN7 admin department, and I did not feel safe going back there. This was also the hotel where the last of the Indian nationals to arrive in South Africa had been lodged by ANN7. I had meant for Cotswold to be a temporary place to stay until I found something safer but just had not had the time to look for an alternative.

I saw a petrol station in the distance; it was the same one that ANN7 cars used to fill up with fuel. But it was lit and crowded, so I felt safe. I walked towards it hoping I could call for help.

But who could I call? I had seen how close Atul was to President Zuma, and so I didn't think the police would be of any help. I doubted they would register a complaint against Atul. I was scared the police would instead expose my location and expose me to more harm.

I then thought of calling the Indian High Commission as soon as I found a phone. But then the High Commissioner, Virendra Gupta, was a Gupta family friend. In my opinion they were very close, and I felt certain that there was no way the High Commissioner would help me.

When I reached the petrol station it was dark, and I was

exhausted and breathless. I walked into the attached store. The two customers inside and the attendant could see immediately that I was not well. I sat on the floor and explained to the store manager that I needed to charge my phone so that I could make a call. After some asking around he was able to bring me a charger. I plugged it in and waited for it to come back on. My mind was in overdrive thinking of where I should go from there. My phone came on, and I was relieved to see a full signal icon on the screen. I got an SMS about the calls I had missed from the time I left the office.

There were five missed calls from Atul. I was very angry. What more did he want? He subjected me to insults, then tried to coerce me into signing a settlement I did not agree to and, after having his bodyguard chase me, he still wanted to call and threaten me.

I called Margriet.

'Margriet, I do not want to have any contact with ANN7 anymore. Please get these people off my back. I am a journalist and not a gangster. I do not want the return ticket to India; I will buy my own ticket. I am not happy with the money you are offering me. I reserve my right to appeal against the settlement you have calculated for me.'

There was silence on the other end. I could understand that she was doing what Atul told her to and did not have a say in the way things had been conducted earlier. I hung up.

I returned Atul's call.

'Mr Gupta, you win today. I cannot fight with people armed with guns. I do not want the air ticket or the money you are offering to pay me now. I will buy my own ticket. I want to go back to India, and I will challenge the settlement legally when I regain my strength. I am sick, I am tired, and I am a thousand miles away from home; I do not want to be subjected to mind games and intimidation anymore.'

'Rajesh, I am worried about you. Where are you? You are

unwell. Let me come to wherever you are and talk to you. Tell me where you are?' I knew Gupta well enough by now and knew that his intention to meet me was not to help me. Just a few minutes before he had had his bodyguards intimidate and chase me.

'After what happened this evening I would be a fool to agree to meet you or Laxmi Goel. What was your intention? Did you think you could force me to sign a settlement I did not agree to?'

'Okay, who do you trust? I will send someone you trust, so that they can safely take you to wherever you want to go. You are unwell. Should I send Sanjay Pandey? Do you trust him?'

I was still sitting on the floor, too weak to even stand up. My hands where trembling, and I felt I could faint at any time. Even so, my suspicions were alerted by this show of concern.

I did not trust Sanjay, but I had no other options. If I called the people I trusted, it would have put them at risk of losing their jobs or worse. All the people I trusted had brought their families and had admitted their children to schools in Midrand. I did not wish to expose them to possible retaliation on my account.

'Okay, send Sanjay. I need to go to the hotel at Blue Hills. Ask him to come alone.'

Sanjay had arrived just days before the launch and was working as the overall production head. His hiring was never discussed with me. We had found a lot of local people who were fit for the job, but Laxmi chose to send his loyalist to the project.

I saw a Toyota Innova drive into the petrol station after a few minutes. I did not come out of the room but stood up to take a closer look.

Sanjay was sitting next to an ANN7 driver; there was no one else in the car. He got out of the car and started looking for me. I waited in the room to check if there were any other cars tailing him. When I could see none, I stepped out of the dark room and walked towards him.

'How are you, Rajesh? We are worried about you,' Sanjay said with a straight face.

'Worried? But Atul and Laxmi just had an armed bodyguard try to force me to sign a settlement they made for me. How can they be worried?'

'Let that become clearer in the car. I will take you home,' he said in a soothing way.

I got in and asked the driver to take me to the Blue Hills area. The driver knew the hotel as he had picked up and dropped ANN7 employees there.

'So what are your plans? When are you going back?' Sanjay asked me.

I was suspicious, certain he would relay any information I gave him to Atul and Laxmi.

'I am too unwell to think of anything. Just take me to the hotel; I will feel better after I have had my medicine and a meal.'

I asked Sanjay to drop me at the gate and leave, but he insisted he would accompany me to my room. I did not want him to know which room I was staying in, but he insisted.

He walked with me to the room. I took my medicine and lay down on the bed. Sanjay stayed in the room and started looking around.

'Where is your luggage, Rajesh? There is no cupboard here; where have you put your passport and valuables?'

I wanted to rest and was almost asleep. I told him I had put them in a safe place.

As soon as I said that I realised he would now assume that the 'safe place' would be the house of my Indian colleagues who were seen as close to me. I pointed vaguely towards the room next door and said, 'This guy stays at the hotel the whole time, so I have asked him to keep my luggage and passport for safety.'

He suggested he take me to get something to eat. I tried to dissuade him, saying that I would rather just sleep, but he insisted

Indentured

we go to McDonald's, as he had something serious to discuss with me. 'Atul has given me some papers for you,' he explained.

'What papers?'

'Come, I will show you over dinner.'

One of the pills Dr Cassim had prescribed was a sedative, and it was making me drowsy. I told Sanjay that, but he insisted I go with him. My sugar level was dropping, and I realised I could do with a meal. I agreed even though I was still filled with misgivings.

'What papers has he given you, and what does he want me to do with them?'

'Don't get angry and anxious, just wait until we get to McDonald's and have something to eat. I will explain everything to you.'

Once we were seated, Sanjay said, 'Atul ji[2] wants you to take the flight back to India the day after tomorrow. He has sent these business class tickets for you. You must leave at noon. He will send a car to take you to the airport, and if you want he will also send a car to stay with you tomorrow for shopping.'

'Why does he want to do that? What is the catch?'

'He has sent this document with me; he wants you to sign it and return it to him through me.'

I took the document from him. It was the same document that Margriet had shown me. The same document I had refused to sign earlier.

'But Sanjay, I have already told them I do not want to sign this document. I intend to challenge this in a South African court as soon as I am medically fit. You can see how exhausted I am now.'

'Look brother, people like you and me never win if we take powerful people on. They will buy the best lawyers and defeat us. The cost of litigation over two or three years is going to kill us. Also, if you take a media house to court, no other media house will

---

2   'Ji' is a gender-neutral honorific suffix to names in many Indian languages.

touch you with a barge pole,' he said biting into his burger.

'Just sign this. It gives you five days' pay and a return flight, and you will leave on good terms with Atul ji and Laxmi ji. You know they are powerful people, both in South Africa and India. Why do you want to put yourself at risk, brother?'

'Sanjay, can you take me back to the hotel?'

As we drove back he asked me again if I would sign.

'Look Sanjay, I told Nazeem Howa and Margriet Coetzee this morning that I need to be paid for working overtime and at least two public holidays. Then there is annual leave that I have accrued, which needs to be paid out. What about the phone calls? I have made thousands of rands worth of phone calls for official work. All these things need to be negotiated. I cannot accept pay from the end of the last payroll cut-off date to the last day I worked. It does not happen like that anywhere in the world. All I am asking for is my legitimate dues.'

'Brother, I understand, the pay issue is something that you are not happy with. And will you take the ticket?'

'If the ticket is conditional on my signing the unfair settlement, I will buy my own ticket and get back home. If it is not conditional, I will think about what to do.'

'I will ask Atul ji and get back to you within an hour,' Sanjay said and left me at the gate.

As I was walking back towards my room in Cotswold Inn that evening, I saw a few unfamiliar faces on the lawn. They were all looking at me. I never saw guests standing on the lawn at that time of the night, and I grew suspicious. The hotel office closes at about six in the evening, and there were no hotel staff to be seen after that. The hotel never had any security guards, and that made matters worse for me.

About three of them followed me, and the remaining one stood near the gate as if to keep watch.

I ran into my room and locked the glass door. I slammed the sliding metal gate shut and locked it too. These men could be armed, but would Atul actually be so stupid as to kill me because of what I thought was a small disagreement?

I had been through two intense sessions of 'hostile environment training' as a journalist reporting from conflict areas across the world. I had been trained to protect myself during situations like these. I switched off all the lights and hid behind the wall of the bathroom. The 6-inch wall could protect me against fire from small arms.

I lay flat on the floor and called Nazeem.

'Hello Rajesh, how are you doing?'

'Not too good. I am surrounded by Atul Gupta's goons in my hotel room. I am lying flat on the floor in the bathroom, and these goons have surrounded the complex.'

'How are you so sure that they are Atul Gupta's people?'

'Because I have faced repeated attempts to coerce me into signing a settlement that I do not want to sign. You are a fair, reasonable man. Can you ask Atul to move these people away from here?'

'I don't know what you are saying; let me come to your hotel and see things for myself. You stay right there; I am coming.'

'It's the Cotswold Inn at Blue Hills.'

'I am at a party with my wife right now. I will drop her home and be there shortly.'

At that time I thought calling Nazeem was the right thing to do. I respected him as a professional. I had established a rapport working closely with him and thought he would surely not approve of attempts to coerce a colleague.

Just then I got a call from Sanjay.

'I spoke with Atul ji, and he says if you take the ticket you will also have to sign the settlement. You cannot take the ticket without signing.'

Atul knew I was vulnerable and unwell, and he wanted to force me to sign a settlement that would make it impossible for me to challenge him legally later.

'Tell him I do not want the ticket. I will buy my own ticket, and I will also not sign the unfair settlement.' I disconnected.

The sedative was now really making me drowsy, but I had to stay alert. I was tired and angry.

After a few minutes, I could hear a car start and drive away. I crawled towards the glass door and peered out. The light on the lawn, which had a motion sensor, came on. I could see that there was no one on the lawn, in the parking area or outside my room now.

I pulled the thick bed cover off the bed and wrapped it around me. I grabbed my cap and phone and switched on all the lights in the room.

I went out, locked the room and hid behind a tree that had a clear view of the main gate and most of the parking area. I was sure they would come back for me.

I called a trusted Indian colleague and asked him to come and pick me up. He had brought a company car home. I asked him to pick me up outside the hotel and give me a call when he was a couple of minutes away, hoping he would arrive before Nazeem.

I moved towards the main gate, opened it with the access key and went outside. It was dark and very cold. I hid behind a tree across the road from the hotel. I felt like a fugitive.

My friend arrived about 20 minutes later. Expecting Nazeem to come the same way and not wanting him to see us together, as I was afraid it might get my colleague into trouble with Atul, I instructed him to drive towards his house with the lights off until he reached the main road.

I felt safer moving away from Blue Hills. I called Nazeem from the car. He did not answer.

Indentured

I called Moegsien Williams, the editor of *The New Age*. I thought, as a journalist and editor himself, he could drill some sense into Atul.

'Moegsien, this is Rajesh. I resigned from ANN7 three days ago, and now I am being subjected to criminal intimidation by Atul Gupta. They are using their bodyguards in the office and people who appear to be hired goons to surround my hotel room to force me to sign the final settlement. I think the settlement violates my rights, and I will not sign it under threat.'

'Where are you right now?'

'I have left my hotel. I am safe for the present, but my safety and life are under threat. I want to report the matter to the editors' guild or the journalists' association. Can you please help me with numbers? I need to make contact with them immediately.'

'Don't worry, Rajesh, I will call Nazeem now and come to see you. Are you at the hotel?'

'I am at a safe place now. Just tell me when you are leaving home, and I will see you at the gate of the hotel. But you must come; my life is under threat here.'

I called Nazeem again. He picked up this time.

'Are you coming to meet me, Nazeem?'

'I will in a bit, but tell me what happened at your meeting with the shareholders?'

I explained the sequence of events to him in great detail.

'So how much money do you want for the settlement?'

'Nazeem, I have already told you that I want only my legitimate dues as per South African laws. The bigger issue now is the threat to my life. I told you how a bunch of people surrounded my room immediately after Sanjay Pandey left. How can any media organisation intimidate its journalists? How can they send goons to make him sign a document? There are civil ways of resolving disputes. If a court says the settlement complies with South African laws, I will accept it. I have a right to take the matter to court.'

'So what do you intend to do?'

'I will talk to the editors' guild and the journalists' associations in the morning and report the abuse, intimidation and trauma that I have been subjected to. If Atul Gupta gets away with doing this to his senior editor, there is no telling how he would treat the rest of the newsroom staff. This is criminal.'

'We will discuss this when we meet. Moegsien and I will come and meet you shortly.'

I knew he was reporting back to Atul about the conversations he was having with me. I had a hunch both Moegsien and Nazeem would not come to meet me. And indeed they did not come that night.

I sat in the car in the parking lot outside my friend's house for a couple of hours and then asked him to drive me back to the hotel. This day seemed to be stretching on for an eternity. I sent SMSes to Nazeem and Moegsien and asked them if they would come to meet me. They did not respond. I spent the rest of the night outside the hotel under a tree, awake, looking out for any sign of danger. The people who had surrounded my room earlier did not come back that night.

I returned to the hotel room at six in the morning. I called a senior South African journalist at ANN7 and asked her to get me the numbers of the head of the South African National Editors' Forum.

I told her about the criminal intimidation I had been subjected to the previous day. She called me back a few minutes later and gave me the number of Amina Frense from the South African National Editors' Forum.

It was early, but I called Amina and told her about my predicament and that I needed urgent help. She assured me that she would pass my number to a few journalists.

'If anything happens to me, Amina, even if it is an accident, I hold the Gupta family and Laxmi Goel responsible for it. They have threatened to harm me, and they have been coercing me into signing a settlement document for the past many hours.'

Next I received a desperate call from one of the Indian journalists at ANN7: 'Laxmi ji wants to talk to you right now. He wants you to forget the past and start afresh. Will you please come to the office and meet him?'

I had told Nazeem and Moegsien about wanting to contact a journalists' forum to complain about the intimidation and abuse I was subjected to by Atul and Laxmi, who probably wanted to prevent this.

'Tell Mr Goel that I will report the matter to the Editors' Forum, and I have no interest in meeting him or working for him anymore. I have my right under law to contest the settlement they are throwing at me, and I will do it when the time comes.'

I started getting calls from the media. *Sunday Times* called me first. A reporter came to the hotel with his photographer for an interview. The usually quiet hotel was full of unknown Indians. There were Indian faces on the lawn, in the dining area and everywhere I went. They were not bothering me, but I was certain that their presence was meant to intimidate me. I remembered seeing some of the same faces at the Gupta residence.

The *Sunday Times* reporter, Werner Swart, and I drove to a nearby café to talk.

I found assurance and support from Charl Blignaut from the *City Press*. He said his newspaper could provide me with a bodyguard if I needed one.

I thanked Charl for his offer but declined and told him that I was not a politician or a Gupta to walk around with a bodyguard. 'My brother and sister journalists of South Africa who believe in the freedom of the media and believe that all journalists deserve to work with respect and dignity will protect me.'

I had come back to the hotel after the *Sunday Times* interview to talk to Charl. Although most of the people I had seen in the morning had left, there remained a couple of Indian consultants who were working with various vendors of ANN7. They followed me wherever I went.

Even as Charl was recording my interview, I was continuously interrupted by calls from former colleagues to the consultants' phones. Mostly they were asking me to return to the office, telling me Laxmi wanted me to stay and work. The consultants would bring their phones to where I was sitting with Charl and his colleague. I gestured for them to go away, but they kept coming back every few minutes. Laxmi was desperate to talk to me.

We had to move twice because of this constant interruption.

I told all my interviewers that if anything happened to me in South Africa or on my return to India, the first people to be investigated should be Atul and Laxmi. I gave them details about the threats and intimidation. This was the only way I could protect myself.

I felt reassured and less vulnerable after every interview. The support I got from the South African media is perhaps the reason I am alive and well today.

Meanwhile, I received an SMS from Nazeem telling me that he would ask the 'shareholders' to offer me a final settlement of 100 000 rand. He said a business class ticket had been booked for me on Ethiopian Airlines and that I should take the flight the next day.

I was amazed at this brazen attempt to lure me away from the media.

I had sent my message to the shareholders. I did not want to work for ANN7, and I clearly did not want the return ticket with strings attached. I did not understand why Laxmi wanted me to stay after the threats, intimidation and abuse I had been subjected to.

Indentured

I felt much more secure after telling my story to the newspapers, and I decided to stay at Cotswold Inn for another night.

Although it was just 8 pm all I wanted to do was sleep.

I wasn't able to order in supper, so I gave up on the idea of eating and, after taking my medication, I went to bed, only waking up at eight the next morning.

To my horror I saw that the door to my room, which I had locked the night before, was now wide open. Entering the corridor, I saw that the door of the room next door was also wide open. I looked in. It was chaos. There were clothes strewn all over the floor; the sheet on the bed was missing.

This was the room that I had told Sanjay that my suitcases were stored. Suresh Kumar was staying there. He was a consultant for Harris, the US company that provided the main broadcast server to ANN7. He had gone out with friends the night before and was now nowhere to be seen.

I asked the staff to call the hotel owner.

He came in startled and immediately called the police. Uday Kumar and Siddharth Rutiya arrived almost immediately, as did Suresh. Uday worked in HR and Siddharth was an accounts manager at ANN7. Quirin Kohler, the acting manager of the hotel, had informed Uday, who'd called Suresh to tell him about the break-in.

Suresh assessed the damage and contents of the room and said both his suitcases were missing as well as every piece of paper, including bills and other proof of expense he had collected for claims. His room had been thoroughly searched; it seemed they were looking for something in particular. It seemed that the robbers must have used the bed sheet to carry away his newly purchased clothes. They had left his old clothes strewn on the floor.

I had only two shirts, two pairs of trousers and two jackets in the room. I slept with my phone under my pillow, so it was safe.

However, my wallet with all my debit cards and the 900 US dollars in it was missing. It had been left on the table near the door.

The robbers had used a crowbar to pry open the doors of both our rooms. Both Suresh and I had forgotten to lock the sliding metal gates in our rooms.

The police took over two hours to arrive. I told the two officers about the threats I had received from Atul and Laxmi the previous day. I also told them that I had misled a senior member of the Gupta management team the day before and told him that my luggage and passport were in the room next door, as I feared there would be an attempt to steal these. Although I did not have any direct evidence, the circumstantial evidence was compelling. I told them I wanted to file a complaint about the wallet that was stolen from my room.

'You were in the room; how come you did not wake up when all this commotion was happening?' the officer asked me.

'I am taking prescription sedatives, and I was very tired.'

The officer was not very keen that I be the person to file a report. He claimed it would be more beneficial and help his investigation if the hotel owner, a South African national, filed the complaint, adding that as I was due to fly out of the country I wouldn't help much. Later, however, he did give me the case number.

I informed all the journalists who had interviewed me about what had happened. I also told them I could not prove that Atul had a role in this, but I felt strongly that he and Laxmi were somehow involved.

Why else would the robbers leave the microwave oven and television sets in the room and run away with two suitcases and all the papers in Suresh's room? They did not take the TV or microwave in my room either, just my wallet with all my cards and all my money. It is a mystery I am told the police have not been able to solve yet.

Was this just general police incompetence, or was there something

Indentured

more sinister in their inability to handle this case efficiently? After all I'd been through, my mind was racing with suspicion.

It was a Sunday, 1 September, and *City Press* carried Charl's story on my dramatic exit from ANN7 as the front page banner headline. *Sunday Times* displayed it prominently on the inside pages too.

Many of my colleagues at ANN7 had not been aware of my exit. I was flooded with calls from them; they wanted to know if they could help in any way. Some offered me a safe place to stay; others wanted me to talk to their friends in the media and shame Atul for what he had done; still others asked me to keep a low profile and exit to a third country other than South Africa or India.

Not wanting to alarm my wife in India, I hadn't filled her in on the events, but she learnt about the incident through reports on the internet and called me. She was worried about my safety and told me that she had booked me on a flight to India the next day. She was frantic. I told her I was safe and did not mention the robbery at the hotel.

More interviews followed that afternoon, and I spoke with Sarah Evans from the *Mail & Guardian* as well as with a team from *The Times*. I finally checked out of Cotswold Inn and moved in with a friend for the night.

The next morning I was on the flight to Delhi via Mumbai.

One

April 2013

AS EXECUTIVE EDITOR, I was part of the team that had just launched News Nation, a 24-hour Hindi-language news station in India. The channel had had a smooth launch and was slowly augmenting its distribution network and starting to get noticed for its content.

It took the team about nine months to launch the channel, with consults from across the world, dry runs for a month and a technical team that delivered as it had promised. It had a great senior management team and was a wonderful place to work.

It was shortly after the launch that I was first approached about a position at ANN7 by a journalist I had known for over a decade and a half.

Dinesh Sharma was a senior journalist at the Indian Zee News and had worked with Laxmi a few years before.

'Would you be interested in a project overseas?'

I had no reason to quit my current job, but I told him I was open

Indentured

to look at the offer. 'Laxmi ji wants to see you and has an offer. He is setting up an English news channel in South Africa with a prominent local company. I have recommended you, as I think you would be ideal to head the editorial operations,' Dinesh said.

The meeting was set up one April afternoon at Laxmi's office in central Delhi. This was the office of his main business venture, Suncity Projects, a real estate company. I was ushered into a plush waiting room and then into Laxmi's chamber. His room was a mix of teak, marble, glass and leather, typical of many Indian businessmen in the real estate sector. Laxmi was a short man in his late 50s. He was dressed in a suit but lacked the finesse and sophistication of new-age Indian businessmen. He spoke Hindi with a rustic accent but with a smattering of English words. He was warm and hospitable and came to the door to meet me.

He always had a string of visitors waiting for him and was in the habit of inviting the next visitor into his room before the last meeting finished. His twin sons darted in and out of his office too.

'I have heard a lot about you, but I think this is the first time we are meeting,' Laxmi said as we shook hands. He and his brothers had jointly set up the highly diversified Essel Group that has interests in broadcasting, publishing, real estate, commodities trading, retail, packaging, television distribution and much more. After a division of the family business assets among the brothers, Laxmi took charge of the real estate business and kept out of broadcasting.

He set up Essel Media, his own broadcasting empire, that would launch television stations in parts of the world where there was no conflict with the broadcast businesses of his brothers.

'I believe Dinesh has told you about the project. It is a joint venture between Essel Media and the Gupta family of South Africa. They are a very prominent business family with roots here in Saharanpur. We have a 35 per cent stake each. The remaining stake as per the law is with a black economic empowerment partner,'

Laxmi told me in Hindi. 'The project will be located in Midrand, halfway between Johannesburg and Pretoria, and it will be equipped with the latest technology and should position itself as a world-class and leading broadcaster of Africa,' he continued. 'Editorial will be balanced, objective and unbiased, just like it was when I ran Zee News. Not like it is now under the new management. There will be no political or commercial interference in the editorial. You know Y P Singh, he has already started work on the project and is currently in South Africa.'

Y P was an engineer who had begun his career with India's public broadcaster a few decades before. After retiring from the state broadcaster, he helped Essel Group's Zee TV set up many regional channels across India. He was seen as someone who could work with a low budget to set up functional news channels. I had worked with him during a previous stint at Zee News from 1996 to 2003. He was a Laxmi Goel loyalist.

'I am considering you for the post of editor,' Laxmi continued. 'I am also talking to two other people. The criteria are simple: I want someone who has worked with an international media outlet and someone who has sound editorial knowledge and understanding of the latest broadcast technology and has been part of launch teams. You are an ideal candidate.'

'Laxmi ji, I am glad that you would consider me for such a wonderful project, but I need a few days to mull this over, if that is okay with you.'

'Well, Rajesh, it is a fantastic opportunity. Should you be selected, you can get out of the rat race here and set up a world-class news channel that will be run as per the highest standards of journalism. There is only one other English news channel currently in South Africa. Your experience working at NDTV, Al Jazeera and TV Today could be put to good use. We will have a largely local team, but you can take a small team of about ten people with you from here.

'We will give you a salary and a one-way ticket and nothing else. The staff from India will stay at a company guest house for three to four weeks. We will also provide contributory medical insurance,' he added.

After that first meeting, I spoke with my wife, Rashmi. She thought it would be good to have an international launch on my curriculum vitae (CV). 'But are you sure about the Essel Group? I mean, I heard there was a bit of trouble with their senior staff.'

'Laxmi Goel has assured me that the editor will have to focus only on editorial matters.'

Laxmi told me that when he headed Zee News there had been a division between the editorial and the business sides. But that changed after his brother took charge and decided that the editorial and business head would be the same person. Laxmi said he had nothing to do with that decision. But he assured me that there would be no such thing at ANN7. However, taking up the offer would mean leaving Rashmi and our two daughters, Ananya and Ahana, behind, at least for the initial few months. Ananya, who was five, and Ahana, three, had never been without me. I was not yet ready to make the decision.

I called a few of my former colleagues to seek their advice on whether I should take up the project and ask if they would want to be part of the team. I met up with Shantanu Chatterjee, a former colleague at the TV Today Network. He had vast experience as an output department head at various international channels, and I was looking at him to head the output team.

Shantanu said I should join and that he would be keen to as well.

Next was Umesh Vohra, an expert on the input function. Umesh had years of top quality production experience and was considered an expert in planning, managing newsgathering resources and world-wide reporter networks. Umesh said he would leave his secure job at the TV Today Network and move if I did. 'It is a leap of faith, Rajesh.'

I called my young colleague Varun Pandey. I had worked with him at NewsX and TV Today in the past. Setting up and running systems and processes on a television newsroom assignment desk was his core strength. He said he would resign if I made the decision to move.

The fourth person I called was my former colleague from New Delhi Television (NDTV), Revati Laul. She said it was a fantastic opportunity but was apprehensive of the Essel Group. She advised me to find out more about the South African partner before I took a decision.

Karun Shawney asked me to take a plunge and said he would join as well. He had decades of experience working as head of production for various leading Indian channels.

I Googled the Gupta family and discovered that they were influential and had interests across varied sectors. The newspaper they owned was seen as pro-government, but I had an assurance that the television channel would be independent.

I called my ex-boss at Al Jazeera, Nick Walshe, to find out what he thought about the project.

Nick had been a consultant with News Nation, and his help and guidance had proved invaluable to the smooth launch we had had there.

He told me to go ahead.

'And would you have time to be a consultant on this project?'

'I have commitments over the next few weeks, but do check with me closer to the launch, and I am sure I will be able to squeeze something in,' he said.

I had been part of the core team that set up many television stations in India, and this was a challenge I thought I just could not miss. I was assured we would get the very latest technology, and I had a great team willing to go with me.

Laxmi called me a few days later from South Africa to find out if I had made a decision.

I told him I thought the project was challenging and would consider if he made me an offer. He asked me to meet him in a couple of days to negotiate salary and terms. I met him again at the Suncity Projects office a few days later. We negotiated a salary, and I was offered the position of editor. I was told I would be issued a visa that would enable me to work in South Africa, a residence permit based on an 'intra-company' transfer.

I was introduced to Uday Kumar from HR, with whom I had worked before; he had been HR vice-president at Zee News for 17 years.

'So Rajesh, now you resign and apply for a temporary South African residence permit as soon as possible,' Laxmi said as he shook my hand. He assured me that it was a permanent position and that the two-year contract was only to satisfy the visa requirements. We would all be given permanent residence permits before our two-year contracts expired.

Leaving News Nation was one of the toughest decisions of my life. I had been part of the team that hired each of the over 250 employees, decided on the work flow, the technology to use, the design of the studio, trained the various teams across different editorial functions and seen the joyous moment of launch.

I handed in my resignation on 15 April and asked to be relieved on 30 April. I joined Infinity Media on 1 May and started working from the Suncity Projects office.

Arun Aggarwal had been hired as the head of business, and he joined a few days after I did. Arun had worked for many years at Zee News, based in Mumbai. Between Arun, Uday and me we hired the key people we were mandated to take from India. Shantanu was to head output, Umesh to head input, Varun to head the assignment desk, Raman Bhatia to be the chief graphic designer, Rahul Singh to head the tapeless video library, and Kalden Ongmu Lachungpa to head the website. Besides these, Laxmi had already hired Jayosh George as the technical head and Roger Joseph Kanjirathingal as junior engineer.

The core team had been identified and offers made. It would then take them a few weeks to be relieved from the organisations they had been working with. In the meanwhile all were asked to apply for visas.

The visa application process was straightforward, and no deviations were allowed. Each applicant was asked to fill out a form and attach a health fitness certificate and a chest X-ray report stating that he or she did not suffer from pulmonary tuberculosis. All were asked to also take a yellow fever shot and attach a copy of the certificate with the form. The applicants were also required to attach a police verification report, which was a character certificate from the local law enforcement.

Applicants were asked to submit the documents and their passports to Laxmi's personal assistant, Laly Thomas. She would scan and send the documents to Ashu Chawla in South Africa.

I was told Ashu was a senior member of the Gupta family's management team. I found out more about him later.

He would send a few documents from South Africa through email to be attached to the applications. Laly would also add a few documents and a bank cheque for the visa processing fee. Ashu would tell Laly what time and date the applicants should go to the South African High Commission to submit their application documents.

All applicants were instructed to meet a person known only as Mr Shakeel and give him Ashu's reference. Only on being told that the applicant was 'sent from Ashu Chawla's office' did Shakeel, High Commission employee, accept applications and give a receipt.

Indentured

Within days, Laly would get a call from Ashu or someone from his office asking that she send someone to Shakeel at the High Commission to pick up the passports with the stamped visas.

'Getting a visa is not a problem at all. Such a visa could take months to get if you went through the prescribed process. But this Ashu Chawla has brilliant contacts with the president's office and is able to get the work done for us in no time,' Laly told me at the Suncity Projects office during one of our meetings.

'I am told by Laxmi ji that it is nothing illegal,' I said.

'I am sure Laxmi ji knows best, but our joint-venture partners believe they have the South African government in their pockets.'

I ignored the last sentence then, although it did worry me. Laly was an executive assistant, so she must have known what she was talking about.

When the day came for me to go to the High Commission to submit my application I was travelling out of Delhi. I told Uday to submit the application on my behalf.

'You had not filled out a column on the form, and Shakeel pointed it out to us. I thought he would ask us to go back after it was completed by the applicant. But he knew we had come through Ashu Chawla, so he asked me to fill the column you had left blank,' Uday told me later.

Like Laly said, all of us got our intra-company transfer temporary residence permits in a matter of days. I had expected an interview or a few questions from the visa officer. There was nothing. A two-year visa was stamped and delivered.

Laxmi assured me that my visa was perfectly legal. But things did not quite add up.

Two

WHILE SOME OF THE CORE group members served their notice period with previous employers or waited for their visas, Arun, Uday, Karun Shawney – head of production – and I left for Johannesburg on 2 June 2013 and arrived on the 3rd.

We were received at O R Tambo airport by Siddharth Rutiya, an accounts manager with Infinity Media. I was surprised to find out that he was barely 24 years old. He was a chartered accountant and the son of a close business associate of Laxmi. This was his second job, and he seemed a little nervous when he met us at the airport.

Our luggage was put into the back of a Toyota Innova and another sedan with *The New Age* printed on it.

Arun and I were to stay at the Infinity Media guest house at Erand Gardens and Karun at the Sahara Computers guest house in Vorna Valley. The guest house at Erand Gardens was where Y P had been staying and the only one that was rented by Essel Media at that time. Uday had already decided to move into the apartment that Siddharth, Jayosh and Roger had rented recently near the Cotswold mall.

The guest house was a sparse apartment in a dull neighbourhood. Krishna Prasad, the skinny Nepalese housekeeper, came to help us carry the luggage up to the second-floor apartment.

The guest house was a mess. The living room had washing lines strung across it with an assortment of towels, underwear and shirts hanging to dry. The first things you saw upon entering were the kitchen counter, the stove and oven.

The living room had two beds, a worn-down couch that could seat three and a fat television set with a satellite television decoder.

'This is depressing,' Arun whispered into my ear as soon as we got in.

'Is this where we will stay, Siddharth?' I asked.

'Yes, sir, your room is to the right here, and Arun ji will stay in the room just next to the living room,' Siddharth said, pointing to the rooms.

Arun and I went to inspect the rooms. They were tiny without any wardrobes or tables, just one small bed each.

'You will have to share this bathroom,' Siddharth said.

I went to inspect the bathroom and was shocked by what I saw. The bathtub was full of unwashed clothes; a bucket stood in the middle of the bathroom with more clothes soaking in soapy water.

There was a wash basin and a dirty mirror.

We were working on a 166-million rand project. Arun and I were shocked at where the head of business and the editor were being made to stay.

While we sat in the living room, Krishna made some tea and *pakodas*[3] for us.

'So, how long have you been here, Krishna?' Arun asked.

---

3   Typical Indian fritter

'I have been here for three months, and my visa is due for renewal. I am here on a tourist visa, so I have to get it extended every few months. Can't you please issue me a work permit that will make things easier for me? Atul ji told me I will get a two-year work permit, but I have not even been asked to apply for one.' The fellow sounded desperate.

'We will talk about it later,' Arun said.

'Krishna is the cook at the guest house,' Siddharth said.

'Why do you say I am the cook? I am also the housekeeper and wash the clothes of everyone who stays here. Before you came here, there were six people staying in these three bedrooms. I also have to cook for all the Indian labourers at the site.' He was referring to the site where the ANN7 offices were being built.

He was really very upset.

'Sir, I was told I would have to just cook at the guest house, but I am made to do so many other things here. My salary is very low compared to what workers get. For the work I do here my uncle in India is paid twenty thousand rupees in cash at Laxmi ji's office in India, and he sends the money to my family in Nepal. I am paid just 300 rand a month here,' Krishna said.

'Why do you need more than that, you eat and stay at the guest house don't you?' Siddharth said, trying to end the conversation.

I found out later that one of Krishna's children was ill and needed regular blood transfusions. He wanted to be with his family but knew that he would never earn enough with his skills in Nepal to afford the treatment his child needed.

'Why are they asking Krishna to work here illegally? Working on a tourist visa is illegal, is it not, Arun?'

'I am sure Atul Gupta knows the laws and is complying with them. Krishna is an illiterate; he wouldn't know. He says Atul Gupta has assured him a work permit. Maybe they are working on one for him,' Arun said, dismissing the conversation.

Siddharth left us at the guest house and went with Karun and Uday to their guest houses.

Arun and I looked at each other as Siddharth left. 'I hope the others find a better place than this,' he said. 'We will have to stay here until we find a place to rent. It is very cheap on their part to make us stay at a place like this. If I had known, I would have asked Laxmi ji to put us up at a hotel.'

For me the worst part about staying at the guest house was the feeling that I was part of the set-up that was exploiting poor Krishna.

After serving us tea, Krishna started making dinner for the three people at the guest house and the 15 Indian labourers and contractors at the site. He was expected to make four meals a day for these people and also buy all the provisions as well as do all the other work at the guest house.

Y P came to the guest house at about nine that evening. He looked tired and disturbed.

We told him we would be starting work the next day and asked him about the status of construction at the site.

'See, the civil work takes its own time, and Atul Gupta is not a man who has too much patience. He wants everything now. Local labour is hard to source, and they work no more than eight hours a day, five days a week. I had a big showdown with him, and now he wants me to pack my bags and go back.'

'What? How can he do that?' Arun asked.

'This man is like that. He gets angry and says things, but I am not going anywhere. He is an impatient, irrational and arrogant man; his brothers are in absolute contrast to him. I will report the matter to our shareholder, Laxmi ji, and ask him to talk to Ajay and Tony Gupta. Laxmi ji will have to ask Atul Gupta to be a little patient with the work.'

'But what happened?'

'It is a very small matter. Atul ji called me to his room today and wanted me to brief him about the progress. As I started briefing him, he accused me of not following all details of the work. He started asking me about shipments and delays in purchasing equipment and what he called the "lack of oversight" at the site. I told him, "Trust me, and I will deliver your channel to you." He erupted like a volcano. Called me all kinds of things and told me to pack my bags and leave.

'I have briefed Laxmi ji about the situation, and he has asked me to stay put here until he resolves the matter with Ajay and Tony Gupta. He wants me to brief you two about the situation and wants you to deal with him in a cool manner and not let him provoke you.'

'But this is bizarre. How can a joint venture operate without trust? I mean, these are still very early days,' I said.

'Laxmi ji wants his team members to take a two-pronged approach. Don't get provoked by Atul Gupta; keep your cool. Laxmi ji will talk to Ajay and Tony Gupta to manage things at the "big picture" level,' Y P explained.

'You guys will have to be careful of a few people here. Aslam Kamal is the chief intelligence gatherer for Atul Gupta. He will hover around and park himself wherever you guys are to get any information he can. He briefs Atul Gupta about the information that he gets. The other person is Atul Gupta's cousin Saurabh Aggarwal. He is the technology guy. He will bug your official laptop and smart phones so none of your communication is safe. If you need to communicate with Laxmi ji or write him a confidential mail, please use a private laptop and internet connection away from the office.'

I was feeling very uneasy.

'But Y P ji, there has to be more trust in a joint venture like this. How can we work under these circumstances? It will be stressful as we move forward,' I said.

'Look, I have briefed Laxmi ji about this. He will come very shortly and resolve the issues with Ajay ji and Tony ji. I am sure this is a temporary thing. As the project moves forward, Atul ji will also learn to trust us more,' Y P tried to assure us.

I did not feel too good about the hostile relations between the partners, but there was no looking back. I knew I had to put my heart and soul into launching the channel and making sure it was done within the timelines. I had made many top professionals resign comfortable jobs to join this venture. There was no way I could allow these issues to daunt me.

'Just look at these as management challenges, we will have to overcome them,' Y P winked and smiled at us.

Just then my phone rang. It was Karun.

'Rajesh, what kind of hell have they put me up at? The bed sheets are stained and stinking, there are cigarette butts all over the room, the toilets are dirty, and there is a family of hideous large rats screeching in the kitchen cupboard. There is no one here to cook and nothing for me to cook with.'

'Karun, let me discuss this, and I'll call you back with a solution,' I said.

It was already late at night. Y P said we could look for a solution in the morning.

'But how do you expect him to spend the night in that rat-infested house? Can we organise a company car to pick him up and get him here at least?' I asked him.

'That will not be possible. I am sure it is not as bad as he is making it out to be. The HR head of the Sahara Group is also staying there. He is a very senior guy,' Y P said.

I called Karun back to ask him to move to a hotel.

'I have already taken a cab and moved in with Uday, Jayosh and Roger at their rented house. How can they expect employees to stay in hellish situations like that, Rajesh?' he asked.

I had no answer. I did not know if the arrangements for the stay of the senior teams were an oversight or a direct result of the simmering mistrust between the two joint-venture partners.

Krishna later told me that the six people who had been staying at the guest house we were in had also been moved to the guest house where Karun had been staying, and that they would stay there for the duration that Arun and I were here.

This included the 55-year-old Om Sharma, the studio fabrication and construction expert, and four labourers from India.

I felt bad for the people we had ousted. We needed to find an apartment to rent so that we could move out at the earliest from here.

I did not have a good feeling about this. I began questioning my decision to come to South Africa. But I was stuck for now. I could not leave before I had launched the channel.

The room I was allotted did not have any space after the three suitcases I was carrying were placed inside. The curtain inside the room was dirty and torn. At least the bed sheet and pillow covers seemed clean. I switched off the lights and tried to sleep. We had to start at 5 am the next day. I could not sleep much that night, thinking about the challenges ahead and the hardships the team I had brought with me could face in the days to come.

Three

THE NEXT DAY WAS the first time I would meet Atul Gupta.

I was up early, but Krishna was already preparing breakfast for 15 people.

He had collected the clothes that were hanging to dry in the living room and piled them on one of the beds. These, he said, would have to be ironed before Mr Singh woke up.

Krishna brought me a cup of tea, and I asked where the labourers and contractors from India lived.

'They were living at the guest house where Karun is staying right now, but they have been shifted to the construction site, so they can live and work there throughout the day. They do not have to worry about anything; their salary is paid to them in cash in India. They stay at the site, and I cook four meals a day for them.

'Sir, but please do something about my work permit. I have been told by Mr Atul Gupta that he will give me a work permit, but it has been months without any forward movement. You are Laxmi ji's representatives. Please help me with this.'

I did not know what to tell him.

We left the guest house on that winter morning at about 6:30. A car already filled with five people arrived to pick us up. I squeezed into the middle row of the Innova with Uday and Karun. Jayosh, Roger and the contractor were in the back row. Arun sat with the driver in the front.

'Rajesh, I had the most horrible night. How can the company put up employees in sub-human conditions? I was really scared about this place, buddy. Uday walked down and brought me to his house. I would have gone mad in that rat-infested hell,' Karun said.

We reached the office at Corporate Park in Midrand about 15 minutes later. We were taken to the first floor and ushered into a small office from where Y P operated. It had a huge desk with a large chair. It was littered with boxes and papers.

'I usually work from here, but I will leave and work from the site from today. You guys take over this place. It has a computer and phone connection and a printer,' he said.

Arun took his place at the large chair; I sat on the smaller chair on the other side of the desk.

I could sense tension in the air as Y P announced that Mr Gupta and the group CEO, Mr Nazeem Howa, would be arriving shortly.

'We will meet them in the boardroom next door. Remember what I told you guys yesterday. Don't get provoked,' Y P warned.

We were summoned shortly afterwards. Y P led the team into the room.

Nazeem sat at the head of the table, and Atul sat to his left; next to him was one of Nazeem's assistants – a young woman with a note pad.

We sat down to Nazeem's right after the greetings and introduction.

'I don't know you guys, but have been told by Laxmi ji that you are experienced professionals. I am told you are the editor and you the business head,' Atul said to Arun and me. 'But Nazeem here feels that we cannot have foreign Indians in those positions. The South African media will make a big issue about it. This is a funny country. So the group CEO will have to be Nazeem Howa, and Arun ji you will have to report to him. We will hire another South African, maybe a woman, who will be your boss, Arun. Rajesh, we will designate you "assistant editor", and you will report to a South African we will appoint.'

Atul clearly had a very different organisation structure to the one Laxmi had discussed with us at the time of our hiring. The tension in the room was palpable. Arun and I did not like the tone in which Atul was speaking to us.

The two joint-venture partners were clearly at odds with each other, but why drag professional managers into their battles?

'Rajesh, you do not look convinced about the re-designation,' Atul said, looking at me.

I thought it prudent to discuss this issue with Laxmi before I told him what I thought about his decision to 're-designate' me.

'I am open to any strategic decisions that both shareholders deem fit,' I said.

'Don't worry. Nazeem here will ensure that you take all the editorial calls; we will have a young blonde South African girl take the designation of "managing editor" and fill the chair. She will be the public face of the channel. I have suggested that we re-designate our HR head, Margriet Coetzee, as managing editor, and you could be the assistant editor. She will be the face and you take the calls,' Atul said.

Atul was a complicated man. He was doing all the talking during that meeting, not allowing Nazeem to speak. He clearly did not want people appointed by Laxmi to take up key positions, but it seemed we were needed to prop up his team.

'Rajesh, this is a very racist country. If we announce you as the editor, the media will hurl allegations at you. It needs a local to take this on. All the media in this country are owned by whites, and they never allow a non-white entity to enter the media industry. We faced so much opposition when we decided to set up a newspaper.

'You saw what has been written about us on the Waterkloof affair. This is a coordinated effort by vested interests to break us. I am sure you have read about it. But I must tell you about the background to the hostile media. We are being attacked only because we dared to enter the media business.'

Atul spent a lot of time justifying the Waterkloof landing incident, which happened just days before our arrival, at this first meeting.

'Our family is close to President Zuma. We have never hidden it. We are a powerful family, and I am sure all the hype around this landing will also pass with time. We land at Air Force stations in India all the time, so what is wrong with landing our guests at an Air Force base here with all due clearances? We are being targeted.

'It was an opportunity for South Africa to showcase itself as a celebrity wedding destination, but they missed the opportunity. We have decided that we will not hold any family weddings in South Africa from now. For the wedding of my sister's son, we will look for venues abroad. As soon as the date is fixed, I will go to Mauritius to select a venue. They do not have this kind of hostile press, and they want to promote tourism. I am sure they will give us any facility we ask for.

'President Zuma knows our family well, and we have deep bonds with his family. We have enough influence in the government to clear our name. And it is not just President Zuma – we have close links with all senior ANC leaders. We are *banias*, we are Indian Jews; we do not keep all our eggs in one basket. Whoever becomes president of South Africa in the years to come, I can assure you he will be our friend.'

Atul loved talking, and he could do so for hours, often repeating points he had already made several times.

'Arun ji, we have a big revenue target for the first year. Do you know about it? I am sure Laxmi ji would have briefed you about it.'

'Yes, he did mention a target of a 100 crore[4] rupees in the first year,' Arun said.

'But you will only have to focus on 25 per cent of this. The remaining amount we will get on our own,' Atul said, winking at Nazeem.

Arun nodded.

Arun and I realised then that an influential member of the government was a shareholder in the company under a black economic empowerment (BEE) deal. But I did not know who it was at that point.

I found out much later about a deal that Atul had made to get 75 crore Indian rupees in the first year of operation. The deal seemed to be to use the president's influence to get various government departments and ministries to pay a part of their advertising budget to ANN7 in the form of advertising.

So the plan was to get 80 crore rupees from various government ministries and break even in the first year. The remaining 20 crore was to be generated by the sales team.

'I am sorry, Nazeem, I discuss revenue in front of your editor. I have a lot of respect for editors and the editorial staff. I am not an intellectual. But I respect intellectuals,' Atul said as I found myself a little confused about the conversation he was having with Arun. He turned to me.

'Rajesh, we are launching the channel in two months. I hope you are prepared?' he asked.

I looked at Y P. I had been part of many launch teams, but I had

---

4   One crore is 10 million.

never heard of launching a station in two months, especially when the studio was still at an early stage of construction, the editorial staff had not been hired and the broadcast equipment not fully ordered, let alone available for fitting.

I smiled. Atul was joking, or he knew nothing about the broadcast business.

I looked at his face again. He was dead serious.

'If we are able to build the studio, get the equipment in place, test it, hire and train the staff and have a month for dry runs, why not? It is possible,' I said in jest.

'See Y P ji, editorial is ready. I do not want any more excuses from you. I want the channel up and running by the end of July.'

Y P nodded with a stern face.

It was clear that Atul missed the intended irony of my comment. He was serious about launching in July and believed this could be achieved by pushing Y P as hard as he could. It seemed to me, reading his body language, that he had nothing but contempt for Y P. He intimidated him like a school bully. He rubbished the issues raised by Y P and called them 'excuses'.

I chose not to add anything else on the issue in the first meeting. The two sides, Atul and Laxmi, had a serious disagreement on the timeline of the project. I did not want to get caught in the crossfire without getting more details about the background to the differences. I was, however, amazed at Atul's ignorance about the processes that go into launching a channel and the timelines. He also did not trust anyone who gave him professional advice, especially if they had been hired by Laxmi.

At this point Aslam Kamal, Atul's Man Friday and the creative head at *The New Age*, walked in accompanied by Saurabh Aggarwal, a Gupta cousin and the information technology head at Infinity Media. Aslam proffered two SIM cards.

'I have bought these for Rajesh ji and Arun ji. They are Cell

C, the plan that allows them to call India at two rupees a minute,' Aslam said with a smile.

'Take their phones and install the SIM cards. Also add them to the WhatsApp user group, and synchronise their phones with our BB network,' Atul said without waiting to explain anything to us or as much as seek our permission.

Saurabh took our phones and left, only returning half an hour later.

'It does not take half an hour to put in the chips and add us to the user group,' Arun told me later.

'Beware of Aslam and Saurabh; they are part of the Gupta intelligence collection team. I am sure Saurabh has bugged your phone; the laptop they have given you is also bugged. Every email, SMS, or conversation you have on your phone or laptop will be known to them now,' said an old-timer at *The New Age* a few days later.

I did not believe him then but soon became aware that Atul seemed to know about the most private conversation, mail or SMS that anyone of us had ever written. By then I regretted not taking him seriously.

'Why did you agree to launching in two months?' I asked Y P after the meeting.

'He is a mad man, he would have started yelling and screaming and shouting at me if I did not agree with his timelines.'

'But, Y P ji, his timelines are impossible. It will take you at least three months to get the studio in place – it is no ordinary studio. It has video walls, multiple sets, the newsroom integrated into it and so many elements. Then you have the production control room [PCR], the servers, the newsroom automation system, the broadcast systems. It will take you a month just to test the systems after integration. It will take us a month to complete the process of hiring. It will take a month for the new employees to serve notices before they can join. We will need a month of training with the new staff on the new systems before we can launch. Clearly, we will have to tell him his timelines are not logical. Why is he in such a hurry anyway?' I asked.

'Atul ji does not trust me; he does not trust anyone. He has set a target for the end of July to launch the channel, and anyone who tries to explain that this is impossible is seen as a work shirker. He has told me to pack my bags and leave when I asked him to trust me on this.

'We will just have to let Laxmi ji handle this for us. He is a shareholder, and he knows television. I am briefing him every step of the way.'

Later that day we sat down to review the project. It was nowhere near ready for an end-of-July launch.

Critical equipment and systems still needed to be ordered.

I tried to figure out why Atul was in a tearing hurry to launch the channel. The only logical answer seemed to be that the earlier he launched, the earlier he would get to air the promised government advertisements. Any delay would mean loss of easy revenue.

Atul knew that many government ministries and departments did not have audiovisual commercials. He planned for the production team to produce these advertisements, at a production fee of course.

So the plan was to derive revenues not only for the airtime sales but also from the audiovisual advertisements that would be produced in-house.

'Please ask our promo team to be ready to make audiovisual spots for clients. They will have to make a lot of these,' Atul told me at a meeting.

But what would a channel that is launched without all the equipment in place, without the systems thoroughly checked and its staff trained look like when it went on air? I had been assured by Laxmi that we would have international trainers train our staff on the latest systems we proposed to purchase, for a month before we even thought of a launch date.

I couldn't sleep that night thinking about the way Atul had planned the launch. I was stuck. I had to go through with it and manage as best I could.

Caught up in the bizarre conversation over the timing of the launch I had almost forgotten that he had demoted me to 'assistant editor'.

But that was the least of my worries. This launch would be a disaster if it went the way he had planned it. I could see that it would bring me in direct confrontation with him, and I knew from this first meeting that it would be a nasty one.

As a professional, I knew I had two things to do.

The first was to try to convince the shareholders to move the launch date forward by at least two months.

The second was to hire and train the staff and get them acquainted with the new equipment as soon as it was installed.

The HR team had not recruited a single staff member at this point, and they were quite clueless about the departments, the newsroom structure and the qualifications and skills required.

We had to start from scratch. The construction work on the studio was a major concern. It was slow and never seemed to have the army of workers needed to finish it, nor did any of the workers seem to have the urgency that the circumstances demanded.

The contract for studio design and construction was given to an Indian set fabricator, Girish Singh. I had met him at Laxmi's office before I left for South Africa. He was quite open to the suggestions I made at that time.

There was no formal contract signed with him nor was the scope of work discussed and agreed upon. It was all a verbal arrangement. He was asked to provide a team of labourers and skilled carpenters from India and to finish the project as quickly as possible.

Indentured

I was surprised to see Laxmi hand him bundles of 1 000 rupee currency notes at a meeting, telling him that this was an advance.

'It is 20 *lakh*[5] rupees; I have given you extra money. If I paid you by cheque, you would have had to pay 30 per cent tax to the government. Now you get to keep that money too. Just make sure the studio is like nothing we have seen before,' Laxmi said, patting his back.

Laxmi was in the real estate business, and I was aware that in India there were a lot of cash transactions in this particular sector. But paying someone an amount over 5 000 rupees in cash clearly violated India's tax laws.

---

5   Two million

Four

THAT FIRST MEETING WITH Atul lasted for about three hours and ended only when lunch was served.

Senior executives on Atul's media team had lunch together in his boardroom every day. Our team from India was never invited to attend this daily ritual. As we sat next door, we heard the loud laughter and animated conversation. Nazeem's laughter was the loudest.

Before we left the room, Atul told us that we were required to attend the review meeting held at eight every morning. It would be headed by Nazeem, and he would attend. From his earlier behaviour I understood that this could only mean that Nazeem would sit at the head of the table and that Atul would hold the floor, talk endlessly and take arbitrary decisions.

'I want a daily review of the project from each one of you. Y P ji, you attend. Rajesh and Arun, you must also attend the meeting. There will be no delays and no excuses for not attending. Please come prepared. If you do not have the information I require at any time, I am known to be a very rude man,' he said with the tone of a feudal lord.

As we stepped out of the meeting, it was clear to me that this was not a place I would like to work for long.

'I was an assistant editor years ago; does he even know the difference between an editor and an assistant editor?' I asked Y P, laughingly.

'Look, we will have a word with Laxmi ji and sort this issue out. I am the project head, and I have never been spoken to in such a manner. There is no clarity on Arun ji's role as well,' he replied.

Just then Y P got a call from Laxmi in India on his cellphone. He let the phone ring once and disconnected. Y P called him back.

I was told later that Laxmi always sent 'missed calls' to people he wanted to talk to. It was cheaper to call from South Africa to India than the other way around.

Y P put the phone on speaker, so all of us could listen to the conversation.

'Laxmi ji, I have Rajesh and Arun with me. They can hear you on speaker,' Y P said.

'How was the first day? I hope you people have settled in. I hope the accommodation is comfortable and you are getting Indian food at the guest house?'

Arun and I looked at each other and smiled.

'Sir, things are okay here. We came to the office today and are slowly settling in. We had a meeting this morning and are getting to understand the issues,' Arun reported.

'Y P, what was discussed in the meeting? Was there any more tough talking by Atul?'

'Sir, he said a lot of things. He said Rajesh and Arun would not directly head editorial and business; that they will have to report to Nazeem through two South African women employees who are to be appointed,' YP explained.

'What? But this is not what we agreed. Arun, have you started taking control of the financial issues from Siddharth?'

'No, sir. Today we spent three hours in the first meeting. I will meet Siddharth now and discuss the issues with him,' Arun said.

'Don't worry about designation. I will sort it out. I will have a word with Tony and Ajay Gupta. They are reasonable people, but this Atul is a tough man to deal with. Don't worry, I am coming to South Africa soon and will fix the issue,' Laxmi promised.

'Rajesh, you must start the recruitment process soon and tie up with the international video news services and do a deal to acquire significant segments of the SABC's library and archives. I hope you remember the conversation we had about the SABC deal.'

'I will start all this at the earliest, Laxmi ji,' I said.

During one of my meetings with Laxmi and Y P in Delhi before I left for South Africa, Laxmi had told me of an elaborate plan to buy archival footage from the SABC, the South African Broadcasting Corporation.

He told me how the Guptas had got a nod from the state broadcaster to buy this valuable archive. The SABC had plans to set up a 24/7 news channel of their own, but they were willing to sell their archives for a sweet deal to the Guptas.

'They have all their archives on mini DV tapes. Their library is not automated or digitised, and it takes them ages to find any footage. We will bring these tapes to our studio and digitise them. So from day one we will have a tapeless library with systems that will make it possible for us to pull out footage within a few seconds.

'We know the people at the SABC, so we will get the footage at a very low rate. You will have to make sure that all the footage of historical importance at the SABC is included in the 100-hour bulk deal we plan to do with them,' Laxmi told me.

Indentured

But the SABC eventually did not allow the footage to be taken away from their office. Rahul Singh, a senior video librarian from India, was sent with mini digital video format tapes and asked to bring back 100 hours of footage from the thousands of tapes at the SABC archives.

He spent about a month going to the SABC every day and sitting at a video editing bay there and transferring all the valuable historical footage the SABC had in its tape library. By the time he resigned and went back to India, he had collected 60 hours of priceless archival footage from the SABC library.

'We are paying them a lump sum to get this footage. We have got a very sweet deal with them. The people at the SABC can be bought for a meal or a drink; they are willing to give away their treasure trove of historical footage for peanuts. They have a clause in the contract that says that we will have to also pay them a "per second" fee every time we air the footage we have taken from them. But they are so stupid, how will they be able to tell what is their footage? How can they audit our use? We will get all their footage forever at just this one-time cost,' Nazeem told Rahul and me when we were discussing the footage transfer later.

Rahul was also told to take anyone he interacts with at the SABC for a drink or meal any time they wanted to when he was at the SABC transferring footage. He was told by Nazeem that this cost would be reimbursed to him.

'Get all of Nelson Mandela's footage, get footage of the atrocities on the blacks during the apartheid years; we can use it to show the young people of today how the whites treated their grandparents and parents. This footage is priceless, and I want you to take as much of it as possible back with you. Even if you get more than 100 hours, get that, we will pay them under the table,' Atul told Rahul during our discussion.

The archival footage at the SABC was indeed of a very high

quality and in my view worth millions of rands. Nazeem, Laxmi and Atul repeatedly told me that the contract with the SABC for this sale favoured ANN7, was drafted by Gupta lawyers and that the price of the footage was 'peanuts' compared to its real value.

Rahul digitised all the footage he got the very same day and catalogued and classified it on the video library system. This meant transferring the footage from tapes to servers. After the footage was tagged and put on the server, ANN7 was able to retrieve and air it in a matter of seconds, something that would take the SABC team hours or even days to do.

I have not been able to figure out why the SABC signed this contract and handed valuable footage shot over decades to a company that had far superior archiving technology and would be a rival to its own proposed 24-hour news channel.

Late that afternoon on the day I first met Atul, I went to HR and helped the team formulate a list of departments and positions. We sat late into the night drawing up a document describing the role of each department in a television newsroom and defining the roles and responsibilities of each of the over 150 employees we intended to hire before the launch. The team had never hired for a television station before and had a tough time understanding the structure, departments and roles.

I also composed two advertisements listing positions available in the editorial and technical departments. These advertisements were placed in *The New Age* and on some websites a few days later.

The HR team started getting applications. It was a trickle at first, but then CVs started pouring in in torrents – hundreds of them a day. Every single day for the next two-and-a-half months, the HR team and I would sit through dozens of interviews and shortlist suitable candidates.

There was no dearth of skilled TV news professionals in South Africa. We got applications from all the major TV stations. But I

Indentured

realised soon enough that the budgets we had planned for most of the positions were well short of what rival companies were paying.

ANN7 did not offer any medical aid or benefits, and that made our package even less attractive for the cream of the applicants wanting to join. I raised the issue with Laxmi. He said he would not raise the salary budget and that we had to find people within those budgets.

'We will have to run the operation on a par with the costs we operate in India. If you look, you will find good people. This is a country with over 25 per cent unemployment,' Laxmi told me over the phone.

The recruitments had to be finalised very soon if the news channel was to launch on the target date set by Atul. Both Laxmi and Atul were unwilling to raise the salary budgets, which were pegged at Indian rates. The option I thought best was to start by filling the junior positions: trainees, assistant producers, junior camera people and video editors.

It was tough to find engineers, newsroom IT professionals, and audio and vision mixers at the rates that were laid down. It was not that South Africa did not have these skills. However, the number of people with these skills was limited, and shareholders at Infinity Media were not willing to even meet the salaries and benefits these people were drawing in companies they were already working with.

I could not understand how a company that was confident of making a 100 crore rupees a year did not want to spend money to get the best professionals available in the country.

However, it soon became clear when I realised that quality of content was not a priority for Atul. He was assured of revenues, and spending on the quality of content was not the name of his game.

I had proposed that Nick Walshe, a senior member of the team that founded Al Jazeera, and his team be hired as consultants to train the young team we were bringing together. Nick had transformed a bunch of young journalists into world-class professionals over a one-month training session.

I had contacted Nick before I left India and asked him to send me a proposal.

When I presented the proposal to Atul, he was dismissive.

'Why should we hire Nick? We can look at any Tom, Dick or Harry. Training journalists is not important. What is there to train anyway? They need to take a camera and shoot,' Gupta told me when I told him about the need to train the young team we were hiring.

Among the applications we received were dozens from senior journalists and technicians. Many were not even considered because Atul thought they were too critical of the government and 'aligned with the DA', the Democratic Alliance, official opposition party in South Africa.

When Nazeem suggested hiring veteran broadcast journalist Debora Patta, his response was vehement.

'She is a white bitch! She is not a journalist, she is a sensationalist. She is a well-known face on TV here, but her aggression is reserved for the government and its ministers. She has an agenda. Nazeem, we should look for someone else.'

Debora did not turn up for a couple of appointments fixed with her at *The New Age* office.

My former colleague from Al Jazeera, Imran Garda, was another journalist whom Nazeem and Atul approached for a senior position.

'He does not have a job now, and we could pay him half of what he was drawing at his last job a year ago. He will be a good face to have on our prime time,' I argued.

Imran politely declined the offer and went on to re-join Al Jazeera.

Atul had very little respect for many of the top South African

Indentured

journalists and editors, particularly because of their reportage on the Waterkloof landing. He would talk for hours about how unethical and petty the media in South Africa was and how *The New Age* was changing the way media reported on the government and the achievements of what he called the 'pro-poor' Zuma government.

But *The New Age* was not beyond reproach. He spoke about and described journalists at *The New Age* in pretty much the same disrespectful tone.

'Rajesh, we have learnt a lot of lessons the hard way at *The New Age*. Many journalists here are blackmailers and work shirkers. Have you seen the way we have put biometrics and cameras everywhere in the office? It is to keep a close eye on each and every employee. With this I get a detailed report of how many minutes each of them spend in the cafeteria or wandering outside the newsroom. If I want to know where any of these people are, I have monitors to tell me. We will have the same systems at ANN7, even more advanced biometrics, access control systems and cameras to keep a close watch on each person in the newsroom.'

I was shocked. As a journalist I could imagine how suffocating this constant surveillance could be. I had never worked in an environment where management kept close tabs on the movement of journalists.

'But do you really need this kind of system for a TV station?' I asked.

'It is important for us to know exactly when they came in, when they went out, how long they spent smoking, how long they spent in the canteen. Also the time spent outside the newsroom is not counted as part of working hours, so if they spent an hour in the cafeteria out of eight hours, they have worked only seven hours that day.

'We cut salaries if journalists do not log the required hours in the office, we have GPS systems fitted in our office cars, and we track the movement of reporters closely. We know if they are not where they have said they are going to. Journalists need to be closely watched, they should never be trusted blindly. I am sorry I have to say this, but you can ask Nazeem; he will tell you the same.'

So I had to hire journalists who would agree to be under constant surveillance and work without any benefits and at salaries that were below the industry average in South Africa.

To add to this, many senior journalists we met had reservations about working for the Guptas. The project was being called 'Gupta TV' in the public domain. This was turning out to be a serious challenge, as many shortlisted senior journalists just did not turn up for final interviews, and many who were given offers just did not pitch for work on the day they were supposed to start.

Most of the people we ended up hiring were young with little or no experience in television journalism. Many of them were fresh out of journalism schools, and their only experience was brief internships with radio stations, newspapers or the SABC.

The process of hiring the first 150 people was tough. I went through hundreds of CVs and rounds of interviews in the next two-and-a-half months. The process of recruitment took many hours each day.

But even as we were handing out offers of employment and asking the newly appointed employees to join, there was no place for them to work. The studio floor was far from complete, and the systems on which they were to work had in some cases not even been ordered or were still weeks away from delivery and installation. Y P's team was under tremendous pressure to deliver the studio and the broadcast system as soon as possible.

Our first review meeting was stressful to say the least.

Atul wanted Y P to give him details of all shipments that were due to come from other parts of the world.

Indentured

'I will check with Siddharth and tell you,' Y P said.

'What do you mean you will check with Siddharth and tell me? As the head of the project you should know all these details. You should be breathing and living these details! What the hell do you mean Siddharth will tell me? He is just an irresponsible little boy. I will tell Laxmi ji that we cannot have a young boy like him look at such responsibilities,' Atul shouted.

Siddharth was called in to the meeting and told to report back within an hour. He had one hour to get all the details about procurements worth millions of dollars from dozens of vendors from half a dozen countries using various modes of transport.

Siddharth was not the superboy Atul wanted him to be.

Atul was also deeply suspicious of ANN7's television distribution company, MultiChoice, and filled me with many conspiracy theories about how they planned to sabotage the launch of ANN7. He was very suspicious of a demand from the company to get a copy of the electronic programme guide, or EPG, a schedule with a brief description of each show that each broadcaster is supposed to supply to its distribution company.

'Rajesh, I want you to prepare for our first meeting with DStv, our enemies at MultiChoice. Arun and you will go to the meeting tomorrow, and I want you to give them a copy of the EPG and make sure that Channel 404 on DStv is allocated to us. But I want to warn you, they are our enemies. They will try everything to see us fail. So make sure we have the EPG with us by the morning review tomorrow.'

Compiling the EPG for the first month after launch was a mammoth exercise.

Most professional television stations brainstorm for weeks and do detailed research of target audience groups and viewing and rating patterns before they lock an EPG. Atul wanted me to produce one overnight and without any research input or support.

In his hurry to launch the channel and eagerness to profit from the revenues he was expecting from day one, he resorted to barking orders at professional managers, expecting obedience and never listening to their advice.

I told him that the EPG needed wider consultation and an understanding of what programming the team wanted to put up. I needed market research and ratings patterns of television news channels for one year before I could come up with an EPG for a South African news channel. I had arrived just a few days before and had very limited knowledge of the market. I suggested we hire a consultancy firm with related experience to get these details for us before we started work on the EPG.

'Why do you want research?' he asked. 'The research companies are all linked to our rivals. They will take money from us and give us the wrong information. You are an experienced journalist. Go with what you know, and ask Nazeem if you need any clarification. He knows the South African media market like no one else. I want the EPG ready by the review meeting tomorrow. If you do not know how to make an EPG, just tell me so.'

Atul had a frown on his face when he said this.

I had been part of many television news channel launches before but had never come across such arrogant ignorance about critical issues like content planning.

The Guptas did not want to follow the time-consuming processes that DStv required in terms of quality checks and technical discussions. The DStv top brass, I was told, were not very happy with being coerced like this.

I decided to use a general model to devise an EPG and sat with Karun Shawney to make one overnight.

Five

THE FIRST MEETING WITH MultiChoice and its digital satellite television service, DStv, was a very strange experience. It was coordinated by Max Magwaza from MultiChoice.

We were told to insist on Channel 404 and take a tough stand on any conditions that the MultiChoice team might set with regards to the launch.

'All the news channels are in the slots after Channel 400. We must get the slot immediately after eNCA. This is critical. MultiChoice are playing politics and want to put us in a slot after 500. In your meetings with MultiChoice, make it very clear to them that we will not accept any channel other than 404. Ajay, my brother, is talking with the highest office in the country to ensure that we get this slot, but you must also push from your level,' Atul told us before we left for the meeting.

eNews Channel Africa was a 24-hour television news network covering South African and African stories. The channel launched in 2008 and was South Africa's first 24-hour news service. Negotiations with MultiChoice were happening at two levels: a pincer approach. On the one hand, Ajay was working to force the MultiChoice CEO to get the 404 slot and, on the other, we were engaged in formal talks with the middle management.

Max from MultiChoice welcomed us in the sprawling reception area of their corporate headquarters. He led us to a boardroom full of his colleagues.

There were representatives from the content, marketing, branding and technical teams. Each with a set of questions. It was clear that the team from MultiChoice did not believe we were technically or editorially prepared to launch a news channel by the end of July. The tension in the room was palpable. They were visibly upset with the political pressure that was being brought to bear on them to launch the channel quickly and on the terms dictated by the Guptas.

'So when do you hope to have the channel on air?' Max asked.

'Very shortly, very very shortly,' Y P replied, not wanting to commit himself to a date.

'How soon will you be able to send us a signal for testing?'

'We can give you the colour bars in a month. Our studio and broadcast centre are at an advanced stage right now. We can start sending you programmes immediately after that,' Y P answered confidently.

I listened with growing disbelief to these promises that I knew we'd never be able to meet.

We were advised that we could not launch until we sent a test signal with our 24-hour programming schedule for a month. Only after testing for a month and finding the quality up to their standards were they prepared to allow us to launch the channel.

The team asked Y P about the schedule for key satellite and broadcast equipment specifications. They were not very happy with the answers. It was clear to them that ANN7 was nowhere close to ready and also that we were in a tearing hurry to launch.

The EPG I had made for them was an ambitious one that offered live programming for 18 hours a day. I knew that we were nowhere close to making that content. We did not have the people, the studio was not complete, and much of the broadcast equipment had not even been ordered at this time.

The team did not even have newsgathering and studio cameras. The cameras had been ordered but would take weeks to be delivered.

The proposed news channel did not yet have an archive, and we would have to store the visuals we had shot on an external hard drive.

Soon after, while chatting with a member of *The New Age* marketing team, I asked why Atul was in such a hurry to launch the channel. Clearly, the channel would never meet the tough criteria set by MultiChoice in the given time frame.

I was told that apparently he had an assurance from a minority shareholder that he would get government advertisements from the day he launched. The commitment was said to run into the millions of rands and he didn't seem to care what the content looked like because he had an assured revenue stream. It was for this reason that he wanted to launch at the earliest and was frustrated by the delay.

I now knew that a hurried launch under threat and pressure was inevitable, and it would be nothing like the launch I had in mind. The lack of emphasis on quality content and proper training was also something I knew would be disastrous.

The bi-weekly meetings with MultiChoice were a farce. Y P and Arun were forced to tell the team lies about the timelines related to the status of broadcast systems and technical equipment. MultiChoice made no commitment about the slot they were going to give ANN7. The Guptas saw a conspiracy in this too.

'Channel 404 is the only vacant slot next to eNCA, but these people will not allocate it to us until we hit them with a stick on their head from the highest office. 405 is Russia Today, and we will be pushed to a slot lower than 410, and no one will watch us,' Atul said.

It was telling how the Guptas were not willing to subject themselves to the quality control and technical checks that MultiChoice wanted, yet were willing to invoke the president's office to put pressure on MultiChoice to give them the 404 slot.

I was told by Nazeem that Imtiaz Patel, then CEO of MultiChoice, had not taken kindly to the incessant prodding through the government that Tony and Ajay were subjecting his team to. From being forced to accept a proposal to accommodate the Guptas' news channel to launching it without checks, the pressure was just getting too much for him.

'Imtiaz Patel will do all he can to make sure that we are never cleared for broadcast, so make sure that in your meetings a technical clearance from them should never be a pre-condition for launch,' Atul told us before one of the regular meetings with MultiChoice.

The morning review meetings were getting tougher and tougher for Y P. Atul was frustrated about the way the construction of the studios was progressing. Y P had not worked in South Africa before and was exasperated with what he experienced as lack of commitment from local contractors and builders who he said would 'vanish for days' and 'underdeliver'. He had brought in about a dozen labourers from India on illegal visas, and they were being made to work day and night. They were paid their wages in India and provided with meals and transport from the various Gupta guest houses they were staying at. After a few weeks, all of them were moved to the site so that they were available to work around the clock.

It was a bit of a sweatshop.

Working conditions at the site were miserable; there was only one toilet outside for all the labourers, who were not allowed to use the toilets in the main building and were made to work for over 15 hours a day on a dust-filled, dimly lit work site.

It was hard to understand why the billionaire owners of ANN7 would not invest a few thousand rand to provide better working conditions for the labourers. It appeared to be sheer exploitation and a violation of all kinds of laws.

I was later told by an Indian staffer at *The New Age* that apart from possibly violating South African labour laws, the Guptas were apparently indulging in visa fraud by getting unskilled and semi-skilled Indian labourers to work at the site. All of them came either on tourist or business visas.

The Guptas seemed to know when the labour department was sending an inspector to the site. All Indians nationals would be moved away, and the inspectors would be taken to lunch afterwards.

'It does not cost money to buy the loyalty of an official in South Africa. All it takes sometimes is a free meal or a drink,' Atul boasted to me once.

The friction between Y P and Atul reached breaking point in the second week of June. Atul demanded that Laxmi come to South Africa and explain the delays in the project to him personally. It was announced that he would make a quick trip and specify a launch date based on his assessment of the problems.

Given his business interests in India, it was not possible for Laxmi to come for more than a few days at a time. He always came when the confrontation between Atul and Y P flared out of control. These were short trips intended only to quickly put out fires. But once he departed, the brokered peace between the two sides was short-lived, and tempers would soon flare up again. It was clear that relations between Atul and Laxmi were at a low. Laxmi Goel called Arun Aggarwal a day before he was to arrive and told him to make arrangements to stay at the guest house should it be necessary.

'Laxmi ji has asked me to come in one of our cars to the airport with you. He's asked me to reserve a room at our guest house, in case he decides not to stay at the Gupta residence. I think Atul must have had an exchange of words with him about the delays,' Arun told me.

Laxmi was related to the Gupta family. His son was married into the family of Rajesh 'Tony' Gupta. He thought he would leverage the support he enjoyed with Tony to resolve problems he had with Atul.

He usually stayed at the Saxonwold residence of the Guptas when he visited South Africa, but this was no ordinary visit. Atul was furious about what he thought were 'delays', and it seemed that it was only a matter of time before he would lose his cool with Laxmi. Y P warned Laxmi about this.

Atul and Ajay Gupta were close, but not as close as Ajay and Tony. Ajay would publically chide Atul and did not think twice before criticising and shooting down Atul's suggestions and proposals. Atul was known for his temper. He did not trust anyone. Not his CEO, not his managers, not even his own extended family.

He was known to shout and scream at employees, overrule decisions taken by professional managers, micro-manage affairs and take decisions at the spur of the moment. Some of these decisions would backfire later.

His keen interest in the personal lives of employees and office gossip is a curious trait.

Decisions on allocation of work to the brothers within the group were taken by the matriarch, the Gupta brothers' mother, Angoori Devi. She is much loved and respected by her sons, and her advice is sought on all big business decisions. She spent most of her time managing the affairs of the palatial family residence. It was her decision, I was told, that Atul was to look after the media business.

The brothers did work together when it was necessary to

swing decisions in their favour, such as getting Channel 404 from MultiChoice.

Arun and I went to O R Tambo airport in Johannesburg to collect Laxmi on the day he arrived. One of Ajay's bodyguards had gone inside the airport to receive him. Laxmi came out of the airport and waved when he saw us.

Arun touched his feet, and I shook his hand.

'Rajesh, I heard Atul Gupta has demoted you. Don't worry, I will get it sorted out. I know you guys are facing a very stressful situation. I will have a word with Ajay and Tony and sort issues out. Don't worry,' he said reassuringly.

His demeanour then was in marked contrast to the threats and tough talk I received just a few weeks later when I resigned as editor of ANN7. 'I will go to the Gupta residence now, freshen up and come to the office after lunch. You gather the key people for a meeting. We will take a few very important decisions today. And cheer up,' Laxmi said before he left.

Ajay, Atul and Laxmi came back that afternoon in a convoy of black 4x4s. With them were half a dozen armed bodyguards, and they quickly called for a formal meeting to take stock of the project. We were all ushered in by *The New Age* creative head Aslam Kamal.

Laxmi sat on a couch with Atul and Ajay next to him. Nazeem, Arun, Karun, Uday and I sat opposite them.

Atul looked very nervous, his eyes darting across the room, scanning the faces of all present.

'So, Laxmi ji, are we within the budget we had calculated before? I am told we have exceeded those budgets. I am okay with exceeding the budgets as long as we get even better equipment than what we had planned,' Ajay said.

'We have overshot the budget by a few *crore* rupees, and we will order the remaining equipment very shortly. We have overshot the budget because we ordered a very expensive jib [a crane-like device

Indentured

with a camera fitted on its arm, used to get moving shots in a studio] at the insistence of Rajesh, and also we have increased the number of cameras,' Laxmi said. It was Laxmi who was responsible for the purchase of equipment for the station from all over the world. He was making payments for these as well as part of the equity that he was bringing in.

'No problem, we can always increase the project budget,' Ajay said with a smile on his face.

Even if he had a disagreement with Laxmi about the cost overruns, he was smart enough not to show it in front of the team.

'Any other issue anyone wants to discuss at this time?' Ajay asked.

'We need more cars very quickly…' Uday began before he was shot down by Atul.

'What kind of a person are you? Are cars issues you need to discuss with the shareholders? You bring the proposal to me first,' Atul said angrily.

'Okay then, I would like to invite you all for dinner at my residence this evening. Please come with thoughts on the launch date for the channel. We cannot afford to delay this project any longer,' Ajay said with a smile and moved out of the room with Laxmi and Atul.

Unlike his brother Atul, Ajay was calmer, more patient and less prone to expressing himself bluntly about an issue. His smile always hid what was on his mind, and he used it to good effect.

The dinner invitation notwithstanding, we were in a grim situation. There was tremendous pressure on Y P to commit to a date in the first week of August. We knew it would be impossible to launch by then. Laxmi, too, wanted to launch at the earliest. It seemed clear that in their minds they were losing money for every day the launch did not happen.

Six

THE MEETING AT THE Guptas' Saxonwold residence later that day in the second week of June was held over dinner, and all Indian nationals attached to the project were invited.

There was a relaxed feel when Arun and I walked into the hall where preparations had been made for both the meeting and dinner.

Ajay sat on a couch next to Laxmi who was leading the informal meeting; Arun, Y P and I sat to their left. Nazeem and Moegsien Williams, the editor of *The New Age*, sat on the right. Atul sat on Ajay's other side, and Tony on another couch near Laxmi.

Other employees sat on couches and chairs placed across the hall from them, which was strewn with kitschy busts and statues. There was an indoor swimming pool at one end of the hall and a bar at the other end.

'None of my brothers touch alcohol. But you will find a well-stocked bar in all our homes and offices to entertain friends and associates. Our late father enjoyed his drink, so this is something we have done in his memory. Please get yourself a drink,' Ajay said, gesturing towards the bar.

Three of the bodyguards we saw regularly in the morning were bar tenders by night. I was told later by Atul that they worked 12-hour shifts and were required to drive, do household work and serve guests, besides protecting family members.

A group of six uniformed young white women where serving snacks.

'So, Mr Singh, when will you give us the studio? It is the second week of June now. Are we all set to launch by the end of July?' Ajay asked with a smile on his face, almost taunting Y P.

'Sir, it is possible… very possible,' Y P said, gulping down his drink.

Once again, it was hard to listen to these empty promises.

'But Mr Singh, the way you are working your words mean nothing,' Atul said, frowning. 'You have no clue about the shipment of equipment, and the site is all over the place. I am told some of the equipment has not even been ordered.'

'Atul ji, let's hear what Y P has to say. He has executed many such projects, and you must be fair to him,' Laxmi pleaded.

'Laxmi ji, many things are not in my hands. But I can assure you if the vendors keep their promise on equipment delivery, and the contractors keep their promise, and I am given more Indian workers, we can meet the target,' Y P said.

'But who has stopped you from bringing in more workers from India? Have you told me how many visas you require? Have you given Ashu Chawla the names? If you give the names and passport details to Ashu he will arrange for a visa in a day. How do you expect us to help you if these things have not been done?' Atul said in a raised voice.

'Stay calm, Atul, we will achieve nothing by screaming and shouting at each other. Mr Singh, send us a list of the people you want to bring in by tomorrow morning. We will bring them in at the earliest,' Ajay intervened, trying to cool down the situation.

Ajay turned to me next.

'Rajesh, Laxmi ji told me that you think many people will not join us because they fear we are going to be pro-ANC and pro-Zuma. Tell them we are not. See, the Waterkloof incident has made us a household name in this country. If the Gupta family launches a news channel, it will be watched. Even our enemies will want to know what we have to say. It is a fantastic opportunity; our reputation will get us eyeballs. We will be one of the top-viewed TV stations in the country from day one.'

'Rajesh, are you ready to roll bulletins as soon as we have the studio and broadcast equipment ready?' Laxmi asked me.

'I propose to start producing a daily half-hour bulletin as soon as the video editors, camera operators, reporters and some of the other editorial staff join. It is imperative that we put the staff through the drill as soon as they join. We will, however, need to hire more cameras and get temporary non-linear edit systems in place. We will package the bulletins on these systems until the production control room is operational,' I said.

'That is brilliant. Are you saying we can have a half-hour bulletin every day as soon as the first of the staff join in a few days? What is the status of the cameras and editing systems, Mr Singh?' Ajay asked.

'We have made payments to the vendor. We will get delivery within a month...' Y P answered, but he was interrupted.

'Why a month? Why not tomorrow? If we have made payments why won't they deliver? These cameras are available over the counter,' Atul said, cutting Y P off mid-sentence.

'These cameras cost just a few thousand dollars. I will get you 10 off the shelf from Singapore tomorrow, Mr Singh. What about the editing systems now?' Ajay asked.

'They will come in about a month, but they can be installed only after the Harris servers are in place, which can happen only after the construction is over and we have a dust-free environment. That may take us a few more weeks,' Y P explained.

'Why are you contradicting yourself? You just said we will have a formal launch in a few weeks. None of your systems are in place. Why are you being so vague?' Atul shot back.

'But Y P ji, we can't just launch immediately after the Harris servers are installed. The system integration and testing will take at least a month. We will look horrible on air with glitches and disruptions if we do not test the servers and systems. Also, none of the people we have hired is familiar with the newsroom automation system ENPS. It will take us at least 15 to 20 days to train a newsroom on the system after full integration and testing,' I said.

'So what are you saying? We should not launch before September?' Atul asked me, frowning again.

'I do not know about September, but unless we carefully consider the precise dates of when the equipment will arrive and be installed, and when the staff will be trained by the various vendors, we should not even talk of a launch date,' I said. 'Also, I have always said that we should have at least a month of 24-hour test bulletins while the journalists are trained in a structured way by international experts. This is important because the employees have never worked on these systems, the work flow is very different, and we are using some very new technology.'

'What is the answer, Mr Singh? I do not know anything about the TV business, I do not know if Rajesh is bluffing or making valid points. He does not seem to think that we will be able to launch in July. Is he right?' Atul asked, turning to Y P, who was clearly very uncomfortable now.

'Look, let us target the second week of August. Let us give them some more time. I am sure by then things will be in place,' Laxmi said, trying to save the situation.

'Yes, second week of August can be achieved,' Y P said, nodding his head.

'So, Mr Williams, what is a good date in the second week of August to launch the channel? You pick the date, and we will go all out to launch by that date.'

Laxmi clearly wanted to shift the heat away from Y P.

'Nine August is Women's Day in South Africa. It is a big public holiday, and we can hope to have a grand opening then,' Moegsien replied.

'That is brilliant. We want 80 per cent of our employees to be women, and there is no day better than 9 August to launch. Brilliant, Moegsien bhai.[6] So let's lock the launch date as the ninth,' Laxmi said with a broad smile on his face.

Y P also managed a meek smile, and the others raised their glasses to the announcement.

I was stunned. I had been part of the core team of many TV news station launches, but I had never seen such decision making. The key personnel, servers, newsroom automation system, studio and newsgathering cameras, editing systems, graphics machines, the PCR (the room where video from various sources, like studio cameras, live feeds coming in from satellite vans or news packages and graphics, are put in sequence and switched for broadcast), master control room (from where the signal is fired for final broadcast and from where commercials and promos are scheduled and spliced into the programming and from where the ticker, or scroll, is fired on the broadcast signal), studios – nothing was ready, and they were planning a launch in about two months.

There had been no serious discussions on content or the kind of programming. It was bizarre. Laxmi, Ajay and Atul were all keen

---

6 Bhai is the Hindi word for brother, a term of respect and endearment.

on a rushed, half-baked launch.

I was looking at the worst channel launch of my career. A launch that could potentially wreck my reputation.

'But Mr Singh, are you confident we will get the studio in working shape, the PCR and broadcast systems up and ready by then? We need a month of dry runs on the full systems before we consider ourselves anywhere close to launch,' I told Y P. I was worried.

'Rajesh, don't worry. We will put everything in place in time. You focus on the editorial and newsgathering side and leave the rest to me,' Y P said with the same confidence he had shown at the meetings with MultiChoice.

He had a team of just three people for the mammoth task: him, the technical head and a trainee. They had not even hired the remaining team. It would take a month from the time offer letters were given before these key personnel could join.

The delay in the construction of the studio, newsroom, and production and master control rooms had another knock-on effect.

Some of the equipment had started arriving and was being stored at a warehouse of the Gupta-owned Sahara Computers.

Part of the agreement with the various vendors was a commitment to train the staff within a stipulated period after the delivery of the equipment. In some cases the time frame for such training was about to expire.

Since the contracts were signed by Laxmi's team, including Y P, Atul did not know about this.

Everyone moved to have dinner immediately after Laxmi announced the launch date.

The Indian buffet was made by the Indian chefs at the Gupta residence, and as a show of hospitality the male children of the house helped serve the food to guests.

Over dinner I told Laxmi that the date was very ambitious. I told him we were not ready to launch a 24-hour channel of the quality and the kind of programming mix we had planned. I told him it was not wise to go ahead without training the employees and giving them at least a month of practice.

He just nodded and told me not to mention this to the Guptas or Nazeem.

'Tell them we will do it. You will get the studio and PCR as per the timelines. Y P Singh has promised us he will deliver the infrastructure and technology by then,' Laxmi said.

'Y P Singh is telling you these things because he is scared of the lashing he will get if he asks Atul Gupta to shift the launch date by a couple of months. We must sit down and decide on a launch date based on realistic timelines related to the construction of the studio, delivery of all the equipment and completion of training of all the staff on the systems. Atul Gupta does not know anything about the timelines on projects like this… We must follow the right process,' I pleaded.

'The time for all that is over. We have to pull out all the stops to launch on 9 August 2013,' Laxmi said curtly.

Seven

THE WATERKLOOF LANDING happened after I had committed to join Infinity Media. I would perhaps have made a more informed decision about working for the Gupta family had the incident happened before I joined.

I could sense the public outrage through the comments on the various news articles about the incident I read on the internet. I was still recruiting for ANN7 in New Delhi in April 2013 when news about the controversial brothers and the unauthorised landing hit the major Indian newspapers.

Following the incident, many Indian journalists who had almost made up their mind to join Infinity Media decided not to. Those who had already resigned from their previous organisations were anxious about the future.

They wanted to know how this incident and the public outrage it had created would impact the Guptas' television venture.

Laxmi, who was in South Africa at that time attending the

wedding, told me that the incident had been blown out of proportion by a hostile media and that it would have no bearing on the project.

I relayed this to those who had just been hired. Most of them were mid-career journalists who had left stable jobs to join this venture. They had put their trust in me. Most of them wanted to relocate their families to South Africa as well.

Even though I had doubts in my mind about the project and its promoters, I realised that I could not pull out of it as I had persuaded some senior Indian television professionals and journalists to sign up with the new venture.

Atul was aware that I would have read reports about the incident when I went in for my first meeting with him at *The New Age* office.

Like Laxmi, he blamed the media for playing up the incident. He claimed his family had the required permission to land the jet, and in the same breath he mentioned the proximity his family enjoyed with President Zuma and his family.

'President Zuma is on our side, he knows our family, and we helped him when he was down and out; he will help us through this as well. You know, top ministers of the Zuma cabinet attended the wedding. This is a direct endorsement for us. The personnel against whom action has been taken will be reinstated very soon. We are an influential family here, and no one can point fingers at us,' Atul boasted.

'We have close relations with everyone in the ANC. If Zuma is ever ousted, I can tell you for sure that the next one in line from the ANC would be close to us as well. We are *banias*, and we know how to keep our business interests protected,' he added.

But despite the tough talk, he said he would never hold another family wedding in South Africa. I recall him telling me at our very first meeting that he was planning the next big wedding in the

Gupta family – that of his sister's son – in Mauritius.

'We will have the engagement in India and the wedding in Mauritius, a country that gives us respect for the millions we are willing to spend. If the South African media projected the event positively, South Africa would have become the next big international capital for glamorous multi-million-rand celebrity weddings.'

He claimed that his initial contact with the Mauritian head of state had been very fruitful, saying that the island had offered to go the extra mile for his family.

'I will go to Mauritius shortly to scout for venues and fix things. We will be away from the nonsense that happens here. The event in Mauritius will be a grand media event.

'We are also looking at India as a possible destination. We can hold a royal wedding in India at the various resorts and royal palaces. I am sure the provincial and central government there will offer us help and support,' he added.

The wedding did eventually take place in India. Spread over a week, the ostentatious event was mostly ignored by the Indian media.

Virendra Gupta, the High Commissioner of India to South Africa, was no relation but a close family friend of the Gupta family. He was a regular visitor to the Gupta residence and at the Gupta media complex in Midrand. He often arrived at the complex in a convoy of cars with the Gupta brothers.

At a meeting at *The New Age* office boardroom while the ANN7 studios were being constructed, the Waterkloof landing, and the media attention it got, was discussed at great length.

Virendra was introduced as 'a close friend of the family' and someone who stood by their side right through the Waterkloof incident and its aftermath.

Ajay and Atul thanked him for his help in dealing with the

backlash that followed the landing and sought his advice on the launch strategy and editorial policy for ANN7.

'I am sure you know that the media here is waiting for you to launch the channel so they can give you the Waterkloof treatment,' Virendra said with a smile. 'You need to make sure that you do not give them a chance to point fingers at you.'

'The Chinese are entering the African media scene in a big way. Have you seen the way they are pumping millions of dollars into [Chinese state broadcaster] CCTV and the coverage of the continent? You must be aggressive like them and counter any negatives that they may have about us,' he added.

Virendra was asked what the editorial and business focus should be.

'You must know your target audience intimately. eNCA and the other local channels keep repeating a lot of the news, and that tends to get irritating. They focus too much on a white audience. You should study their weaknesses and then come out with a product that the viewers find refreshing. I am sure it will not be too difficult to beat them. If you get the ratings, the business will follow,' he advised.

'Virendra ji, you talk like a businessman and not like a diplomat. You clearly have deep insights into this business,' Atul complimented him.

'I am a *bania* like you; business is in our blood. These are things we pick up following the businesses of our relatives when we are growing up,' Virendra said with a smile.

Atul seemed to enjoy the notoriety that the Waterkloof landing gave him. He would often amuse young staff at restaurants and ushers at conferences by introducing himself as 'Atul Gupta of Waterkloof fame'.

I was told by a senior member of *The New Age*'s advertising and sales team that advertising in the paper was seriously impacted after the scandal. Revenues dipped to an all-time low. He told me about how the already poor circulation was also further impacted, with many copies being returned unsold.

The New Age refused to let any credible external agency audit its circulation, and its revenue figures were also kept a closely guarded secret. Its claimed circulation has never been verified by any independent agency.

The only saving grace for the paper was the regular *New Age* Business Briefing broadcast on SABC. This was a cash cow. Atul twisted arms at the SABC to give him a morning slot for a question-and-answer format breakfast show featuring key national and provincial ministers and officials.

Nazeem told me that each of the shows earned them up to 1.8 million rand. The paper's marketing team was always busy booking ministers and venues for multiple broadcasts. Many times it was done at no expense to the paper, as the ministries paid for hiring the venues and the hospitality, and the SABC footed the costs for broadcasting. *The New Age* earned from not just the sale of tickets but also from various government departments.

Atul boasted to me once that he could get any national or provincial minister he wanted for the show.

This was an excellent networking opportunity for Atul and his close coterie who sat at the high table with the guests and officials. *The New Age* Business Briefing was used extensively by Atul as a public relations exercise since the Waterkloof scandal.

All the guests were taken to a holding area at the venue before the broadcast of *The New Age* Business Briefing began. Atul would closet himself with them, and would be joined by Nazeem and Moegsien. I was asked to join on a few occasions.

These meetings were almost always focused on seeking advertisements from the ministries or departments they represented and clarifying various issues raised by the South African media, including the Waterkloof scandal.

The same person in the marketing team who had told me about advertisers pulling out of *The New Age* said it would be tough to get any advertisements from the private sector on ANN7 because of the Guptas' reputation and lack of credibility since the Waterkloof scandal.

The decline in advertising revenue was something that on the surface did not seem to worry Atul or the senior management at *The New Age*. It was discussed during meetings with President Zuma as well.

The Waterkloof scandal had clearly had a deep impact on Atul, despite him joking about it in public. During a meeting, discussions veered towards the incident and how the Gupta family had been 'humiliated' and slighted by the media and a 'few inimical officials'.

'One day these officials will know the power of the Gupta family. Right now we are forced to be on the defensive, but that will not always be the case. We will remember these people and will definitely teach them a lesson when we can, and I am sure we will one day. Young children in my family have been scarred for life, and that is not something anyone in my position is likely to forget or forgive,' he told me.

He was referring to how the young bride and groom were put through what he called 'trauma' by his 'business and political rivals'.

The family kept a close watch on all media reports related to what had become known as 'Guptagate', and Atul personally kept tabs on all related tweets. He was especially interested in what opinion makers, talk-show hosts, journalists and celebrities had to say.

Every morning a dossier of news clippings was prepared for him, and he spent a lot of time reading through these and discussing them at length with Nazeem and Moegsien.

His obsession with the issue was such that when the channel was looking for a host for a weekly half-hour aggressive one-on-one interview show, he would offer himself as a subject for a role-play scenario. Potential candidates would have to grill him on a three camera set-up on the Guptagate issue.

'Let your questions be as hard as you can make them. Your interview with me will be a test of your research and interview skills,' he told a candidate.

The candidates always thought it unwise to upset their potential employer and would invariably ask questions that were not very harsh. When President Zuma suggested that his old confidant and former government spokesperson Jimmy Manyi be made the host for such a show, Atul put him through the test too.

It was strange how Atul steered clear of media questions and had a family spokesman and Nazeem answer questions related to Guptagate, yet he enjoyed answering questions in the mock interviews with eager-to-please job seekers.

He would have the footage edited and take it home to show his family. But he insisted that no one else could access it. The chips the interviews were recorded on had to be formatted and the footage deleted by the camera crew. As soon as the footage was digitised, his employees from India would check to ensure it could not be accessed.

The edited interviews were then deleted from the editor's laptop.

In the mock interviews, Atul gave long answers to the questions, justifying the landing, arguing that the groom's party had approached the Indian High Commission for permission to land and that the family, especially the young bride and groom, were put through an ordeal.

All interviewers, including Jimmy, had no option but to allow Atul to take his own time answering the questions, none of them dared to interject or cross question Atul.

Indentured

Atul always really seemed to enjoy these interviews even though he continually said that the interviewers were too soft and that he wanted the programme to be hosted by a journalist who could stump him with tough questions.

Even Jimmy was branded as too soft by Atul.

'He is a good friend of my brother Tony and hesitates to ask me tough questions. Probably he respects me as a friend's elder brother. But he has to be tough.'

Eight

AFTER ONE OF THE morning review meetings, Arun and I were told by Atul to prepare a presentation on ANN7 for a top government official.

'You must not discuss this meeting with anyone; get the presentation ready as soon as possible. See if you can make it in the next hour. Aslam is an expert in making presentations; he will help you with designing pages and making a glossy spiral-bound document.'

Aslam Kamal was the creative head at *The New Age*.

Atul then called Aslam and shot instructions at him in Hindi. 'Use your magic to dress up the text that Rajesh will give you, like a bride. Use glossy paper and make a colourful folder. Pick up good photos from the internet and Photoshop and use the logo. Baba should be happy to see this. We will go to meet Number 9 any time over the next few days, so do it as soon as you get the text. I want you to make three copies, one for Number 9, and two for us to keep handy. Don't make any extra copies, and destroy any pages that are printed in error.'

Arun and I were amused by the detailed instructions Atul gave for something as simple as printing a presentation.

'We call him Baba,'[7] he said as soon as he got off the phone with Aslam. He was speaking to us in whispers, looking around to see if anyone was within earshot.

He asked us never to mention the official by name in any conversations we had over the phone. He claimed his phone was tapped and that it was possible that our phones were tapped by government agencies too.

Baba, he told us, would not want the South African media to know about our meeting or his association with ANN7. 'He is close to us, but we do not want to make that too obvious,' he said.

'We call the *Rashtrapati*[8] Baba. That is what people who know him call him. He was referred to as Number 9 when he was in the intelligence wing of the ANC. You must refer to him as Number 9 in all your conversations and telephone calls about this meeting. That will be our code word for him,' he continued in a hushed tone.

'When do we meet Number 9? Do we have an appointment yet?' I asked.

'He is travelling now; we will meet him as soon as he is in Pretoria,' Atul answered.

Gupta always spoke about President Zuma with the familiarity of someone who has known him for years. He told us how his family knew Baba even before he became president... even before 'anyone thought he could be president'.

'He respects my mother a lot, and he came to our house to seek her blessing before the last elections. He sits with her for the *pujas*[9]

---
7   Baba means father in isiZulu.
8   *Rashtrapati* is the Hindi word for president.
9   Hindu ritual worship

she performs,' Atul told me once.

'We supported him when no one cared to look at him. Before the last elections his opponents accused him of rape and corruption and made all kinds of charges. Most of his friends deserted him then. The Gupta family stood by him until he came out victorious. He would often come to our house and meet Ajay ji and me. Look where that support has brought him – today he is the president.'

'So what is on the agenda? Is there a formal agenda for the meeting, or do we just meet him and give him a copy of the presentation?' I asked.

'What do you mean give him a copy; you will have to explain the contents of the presentation in detail… None of us know about this. We will meet him for two hours and tell him about ANN7 and the benefits it will bring the country and how it will change the media landscape of South Africa.'

I found this amusing. Which head of state would have two hours to listen to a presentation on a proposed private TV news station?

Arun and I went back to our room and started putting together a presentation. I opened my laptop and started typing the text for the presentation, basic stuff that spelled out my understanding of the unique selling propositions of the station. I was asked to take the editorial vision from *The New Age*'s website and make changes for television for the time being.

I began keying in the basic differentiators:
- We are the youngest, and arguably the most technologically advanced 24/7 television news station in South Africa.
- We have newsgathering teams spread across South Africa and the African continent. We will bring you the latest news and updates as they happen around the clock.
- This is possible using the latest newsroom automation system, cutting-edge newsgathering technology, the best

Indentured

graphics machines and a network of the best, sharpest young journalists and experienced editors.
- Headquartered in Midrand, we bring you news from across South Africa and Africa like no other network.
- Out integrated newsroom and studios are the very best in their class, equipped with the very latest HD equipment.
- State-of-the-art robotic cameras, jibs, broadcast cameras, video walls, editing systems and the latest video and audio mixing equipment ensure that each news bulletin and programme is produced to the very best international standards.

Editorial vision
- To present a wide range of news and information in a bold, accurate and balanced manner.
- To be critical but fair and constructive.
- To raise awareness and consciousness around issues affecting the people of South Africa and the continent.
- To celebrate the achievements of a united South Africa.
- We are committed to connecting and informing communities across a united South Africa and beyond.
- Our signature voice is one of optimism.
- We are unashamedly pro-South Africa in coverage of its institutions, including the public sector but critical of them when their actions discriminate against the person on the street.

Current status
The project is at an advanced stage of execution and a few weeks away from completion.

The state-of-the-art studio and newsroom will soon be ready for broadcast.

> The station is finalising recruitment of seasoned television news professionals.

ANN7 was the only television news station to be based in Midrand and proposed to have the largest number of bureaus, reporters and live sources, such as outside broadcast vans, in South Africa and Africa. The studio in Midrand would technically be able to receive news and live reports from many more locations compared to our rivals.

I mailed the bullet-point list to Aslam with copies to Arun, Atul and Nazeem. Aslam got back to me within an hour with copies of the presentation.

As Atul instructed him, he had 'dressed it up like a bride' with digitally manipulated pictures picked up from the internet, and the ANN7 logo.

'Are you happy with the way it looks? I will try and get better pictures and will improve on this first version,' he said.

I told him I was okay with the document. It looked kitschy, but it did convey the points that would differentiate the proposed news channel from its rivals.

Aslam then took it to Nazeem and Atul for their approval.

It had been more than two weeks since Arun and I had landed from India, and we spent long hours sitting in review meetings, recruitment interviews, technology and shipment reviews and discussions. Atul would dominate these discussions, which often lasted two to three hours at a stretch.

Arun was getting frustrated at how he, despite being the head of business, appointed by Essel Media, had little say in the finances of the company. For every small expense, he was referred to a close confidant of Ajay who kept a tight hold on the finances. Even a small expense could not be committed to without her approval.

It was difficult to pin her down, as she was always in 'meetings' and would seldom return his calls.

Indentured

Two days had gone by since we had been told about the meeting with Number 9, and there was still no talk of when we would meet with the president.

Then, on one Saturday, 21 June at about 11 pm, when we had just returned home from office, I got a call from Atul informing me that President Zuma would return the following morning, and we had an appointment with him at 9:30 am.

I had moved out of the guest house by then and into an apartment that I shared with Arun. I woke up early and made tea.

Arun came out of his room in a smart green suit.

'So we are meeting the big man today,' he said, almost taunting me to come up with a humorous retort.

'Yes, we are meeting the big man for two hours today,' I said. 'Let's finish our tea and get to the office quickly. I don't want us to be responsible for delaying the meeting.'

I took the apartment keys out of my pocket and pointed them towards the door. 'The driver is waiting downstairs.'

We reached the Midrand headquarters of *The New Age* in about 15 minutes.

We worked for a couple of hours before Aslam called to tell us that a car from the Gupta fleet had arrived to take Arun and me to Pretoria.

'Please leave immediately, and take the three copies of the presentation with you, Rajesh ji. Ajay ji, Atul ji, Nazeem ji and Mr Williams will leave in a convoy shortly. I have sent your vehicle number and details to Ashu Chawla, he will be waiting for you at the president's residence.'

Ashu was the CEO of the Gupta-owned Sahara Computers. He had lived in South Africa for many years and was the Guptas' point man for any coordination with the president and the South African government. He was particularly close to President Zuma's son Duduzane.

I had heard his name mentioned for the first time when I was asked to apply for my temporary residence permit under the intra-company transfer process before I left India for South Africa.

'It can take months to get a South African work permit. It is a cumbersome process. We have to advertise the position in South African newspapers and then wait for six months, after which we provide evidence that we have not found a suitable local candidate. Only then can we start the process of getting a work permit. Even so, if there is an official who does not agree, the request for a work permit can still be rejected,' Laxmi had told me right after I signed the contract to work for Infinity Media.

'But Ashu ji is a genius, and he has found a way around it. We will show the visas of people going to work in South Africa as intra-company transfer. Just fill in the visa form, get police and medical clearance and get back to my office. My office will issue papers certifying that you are an employee of Essel Media being transferred to South Africa,' Laxmi added.

'But all the people I have recruited to be the core team to launch ANN7 have got contracts from Infinity Media and not Essel Media. They have never worked for Essel Media. I hope this is not illegal?' I asked.

'Absolutely legal, Rajesh. What rubbish are you thinking? Trust me, Ashu Chawla will tell Shakeel at the South African High Commission to accept your application forms. Shakeel and his bosses at the visa section have a message from the South African president's office to expedite the visas. Do you think the president would do something illegal?'

Uday Kumar from HR went to the High Commission directly without informing Ashu a day later.

The High Commission refused him entry, the reception connected him to the visa section, and the guy who picked up the phone told him, 'There is no Shakeel at the visa section.'

Laxmi was very upset when he found out. He sat Uday down and read out the rules for applying for a visa in the future.

'Look Uday, I am upset that you would make such a stupid mistake. You should inform Ashu ji, and only when he tells you the appointed date and time should you go or send anyone to the High Commission.

'It is not simple. They have to speak with the most senior people in government, and only after that is a message sent to the High Commission to accept the documents and process them without creating a fuss,' Laxmi said in a tone that was not his usual polite one.

So it was clear to me very early on, even before I ever met him, that Ashu could pull strings in the government. He was close to the president and had a reputation for getting the toughest jobs done expeditiously for the Guptas.

When Arun and I went to the car, we heard 'Ram Ram', a greeting popular in North India's small towns and villages, curiously from one of the Guptas' white drivers.

An overwhelming majority of the personal employees that the Guptas had were white. This always baffled me a bit. For all the talk Atul gave us about his 'objective' to empower the 'poor and suffering black population' that was still 'being crushed under economic apartheid', I did not see a single black employee during my various visits to their residence. The chefs were Indian nationals, the bodyguards were mostly white, and so were the people who served food to the guests.

The driver politely changed the radio station to Lotus FM, which played music in various Indian languages. There was a Gujarati Hindu prayer on. I am not religiously inclined and asked him to change to any radio station he preferred.

It was an easy journey from Midrand to Pretoria that Sunday morning, as the road was free of weekday traffic. Ashu kept calling every few minutes to find out where we were, and the driver would give him our exact coordinates.

We reached the main gate of the president's residential compound and were stopped at the security checkpoint.

Compared to my experience as a journalist in the United States, UK, India, Afghanistan and even post-conflict Sri Lanka, the security at President Zuma's official residence was really very lax.

Ashu had conveyed the car's registration number, and the driver was waved in without any fuss. The security personnel did peer into the car as we passed by, but they did not ask us for any identification, although Arun and I were carrying our Indian passports just in case.

The car drove to the front stoep of the main building and dropped us at the entrance. The driver then parked right in front of the stoep among about a dozen other cars.

'The president must be having a busy Sunday,' Arun whispered to me.

We were ushered into a well-appointed room to the extreme right of the entrance. There was no frisking, we were not asked to pass through metal detectors and were not required to give our names and details to any of the security personnel. We just walked in. I was carrying my cellphone and my laptop as well as the three copies of the spiral-bound presentation that Atul had wanted to be printed and bound: one for President Zuma, one for Ajay and one for me to keep in my hand while I made the presentation.

Electronic devices are generally not allowed to be carried for such meetings and even when they are allowed they are thoroughly screened by security personnel. I could not see any X-ray machines at the venue. I could not figure out if this was special treatment for the Gupta delegation, or if the security was generally of a low standard.

Ashu was waiting in the room when we entered. This was Arun and my first meeting with him.

Indentured

Ashu was a reticent man in his mid-forties. He was not very outgoing and seemed very preoccupied. He gave us a limp handshake and went back to the corner of the room opposite the door at the far end. His phone was charging, and he was constantly sending and receiving messages.

'When are the others joining us?' I asked him by way of making polite conversation.

He gave me a bit of a smile and continued to fiddle with his phone.

The room had a shelf with a neat collection of leather-bound books; there was a television set mounted on the wall at the far end, a coffee table in the middle with couches around it and ornate chairs in each corner.

Ashu seemed worried.

While the place seemed like a waiting room, there was no one else there, only the delegation from the Guptas. I had seen many cars parked outside; surely there were more visitors? It soon became clear to me that we were not packed into a general 'visitors' room' and that this was a space specially reserved for us.

There was a knock on the door. Ashu jumped up. It was a member of staff from the president's office who came in to ask if we would like 'water, tea or coffee'.

'No, thank you very much,' Ashu decided for all of us. Arun and I nodded politely in agreement.

I was wondering why the others were not here if we had an appointment at 9:30. It was already 10. Ashu's body language made it clear that something was amiss.

After another half hour passed, the door opened, and the remaining members of the delegation entered.

Atul entered first, dressed in a dark suit, followed by Ajay in casual trousers and jacket. Nazeem and Moegsien appeared in their usual smart suits and ties.

Ashu sprang to his feet and rushed towards the door, bowing to touch Ajay's feet. He then moved quickly and touched Atul's feet.

Ajay acknowledged this gesture of respect like any North Indian feudal lord would; he made a half-hearted attempt to stop him.

'There are a lot of visitors today, sir, but we have been told he will come and meet us soon. Please sit, sir,' Ashu told Ajay.

The two chairs closest to the entrance were reserved, I was told by Nazeem, for the president and the head of our delegation, Moegsien.

Nazeem sat on the couch near the entrance, facing the chair reserved for the president, and Ajay sat beside him.

Arun and I sat on the couch opposite them, with me next to Moegsien.

Atul sat on the chair near the television. Ashu sat in the corner opposite Atul, fiddling with his phone, which was still charging.

The staff member from the president's office came in again and asked if we needed any drinks. We asked for various beverages, which were soon served.

'You journalists have no issues taking advantage of hospitality paid by the taxpayer?' joked Atul.

'Why? I pay taxes here in South Africa. Why should we not?' I asked him, only half-joking myself.

'I was only kidding. You know we have paid taxes for all our companies from the day we started our business. Ajay ji has a philosophy about taxes. When God has given us so much wealth, why should we do something as petty as not pay taxes and always be scared of being caught?' he replied.

He looked at Arun and said, 'You are a chartered accountant. You know how it is in India. All the respectable companies maintain two books. One for internal use, and one for the tax department. We have never done that.'

It was now about 20 minutes since Ajay had come in, and he was getting visibly impatient. He turned to Ashu and made a gesture. Immediately Ashu left his phone and went out. He came back a few minutes later.

'Ajay ji, there will be a further delay. I am told he is in some long meetings with ministers. We have been asked to wait,' Ashu said.

'You know I hate to wait, Ashu ji. Please tell them we will have to leave if he does not have time for us today,' he said. I could tell Ajay was not his calm self now.

Ashu again left the room and did not come back for quite a while.

While he was out of the room, Ajay started explaining the origin of the channel name. 'President Zuma suggested we name the news channel "Africa News Network" in the last meeting we had with him on the issue. The name was already taken, so we decided to call it "Africa News Network 7". We must make the president feel important, and tell him that we are taking suggestions given by him seriously. He will like it if we seek suggestions from him on how to run the news channel. He would like to see us as his own channel. We do not have to implement all his suggestions, but he would like it if we ask him for advice.'

Atul then took out the TV remote and switched to the Indian news channel New Delhi Television, NDTV.

'We want all the graphics on our channel like NDTV. We should have the graphics at the top and the bottom of the screen. There should be many layers. The people of South Africa want a screen that keeps moving and updating. They do not get that with eNCA.'

I tried explaining to him how it was considered less sophisticated to have too many graphic bands and elements on the screen, how it would be better to have a cleaner screen with a graphic band only in the lower third of the screen. This was not what he wanted to hear.

'I want the screen to be cluttered; we must dazzle our viewers with as many elements as we can.'

It was past noon now, and Atul was getting very impatient.

Ashu, who had came back, was sent out again to inform the president's people that we would be leaving. 'We will come back another day for the presentation,' Atul said.

Ashu left the room and returned within a few minutes.

'Ajay ji, President Zuma has sent word that he will come out of the meeting and see us for a while. He wants us to wait,' Ashu told Ajay.

Even as he was speaking, President Zuma entered the room.

'I am very sorry about the delay. I was away from Pretoria and there are many issues my ministers want to discuss with me,' President Zuma said as he came into the room, alone, with a broad smile on his face.

He was not as tall as I thought he would be. I could sense from his informal demeanour that he knew the brothers quite well.

Ajay introduced me and Arun.

'This is Rajesh Sundaram. He is the editor of the television project, and this is Arun Aggarwal. Arun ji is the business head. They have both come from India recently and have many years of experience working with large international networks. You know the other gentlemen.'

'I soon have to go back to the meeting I left behind. I know there are a lot of things to discuss, but like they say in Zulu we will just skin the animal today. We must leave the rest for later,' President Zuma said.

'Sir, I will ask Rajesh to give you a quick overview of the project. He will answer any questions you may have, and then we will ask the TV team to leave, and we can discuss issues related to the newspaper,' Ajay said, pointing to me.

I handed President Zuma a copy of the presentation.

'See the logo on the presentation, sir, it is ANN7. Like you said we are calling the channel Africa News Network. We are following all the things you told us, sir,' Ajay told President Zuma, and pointed to the logo.

The president seemed impressed. He smiled at Ajay in acknowledgement.

'This will be the most technologically advanced television news station in South Africa. The broadcast, newsroom automation and production systems we have are used by the top news networks of the world. Our newsgathering reach will be the widest among our peers, with bureaus, studios and live sources proposed in every province. We will also have a network of correspondents across major African and world capitals. Our newsgathering team will be predominantly female and young. We will train our journalists and technical staff to the best international standards,' I said as President Zuma flipped through the bound pages of the presentation, stopping occasionally to read.

I explained the programming mix and the emphasis on provincial news through two provincial news bulletins a day, the daily Africa bulletin and half-hour bulletins on sports, entertainment and lifestyle.

He listened intently and did not seem impatient to get back to the meeting he had left midway.

I explained to him how the integration of the newsroom and main studio, and placing the main anchors' desk on a revolving platform, would give every bulletin and time band a different look. I told him about the various visual elements on the news floor, the robotic cameras and the state-of-the-art PCR.

'Please leave a copy of the presentation with me. I will study it in detail and will get back to you with input in a couple of weeks after President Obama's visit when we meet again. It looks good now. I think you should keep the funny shows out. Lampooning politicians for cheap humour is not news. I hate the one they have on eNCA,' Zuma told me.

'The news on eNCA is repeated a lot, and that irritates the audience. You seem to have a broad programming mix, so you will not have to repeat so much. No bulletin should be repeated, it should be served fresh,' he added.

'Sir, now we will discuss the newspaper and commercials. I will ask my colleagues from TV to leave,' Ajay said, looking at us.

As we rose to leave, President Zuma got up too and warmly shook our hands. He then walked us to the door and shook hands again before we left.

All three meetings I had with President Zuma ended this way. Nazeem, Moegsien, Ajay and Atul stayed on. I was told later by a member of *The New Age*'s marketing team that these discussions were crucial for the paper to get government advertising and bring hard-to-convince ministers and officials in as guests on *The New Age* Business Briefing.

After the Waterkloof scandal, some ministers and officials seemed reluctant to be seen in public with Atul or on a platform hosted by his newspaper. These ministers and officials were convinced after a nudge from the president, Atul told me.

The bad press and public outcry following the incident did not seem to have made any difference to the relationship between President Zuma and the Gupta brothers. In the three meetings with President Zuma that I was a part of, the two brothers bonded well with the president and joked occasionally about the scandal. It was like nothing had happened.

The brothers had fairly free access to the president's residence, and Zuma left his ministers waiting for hours to attend meetings with the Guptas.

Atul once showed me newspaper clippings of President Zuma defending his friendship with the Gupta family in parliament. 'Zuma, who was forced to publicly defend his relations with the

Guptas for the first time since the plane-landing scandal, dismissed all allegations against him in relation to the Guptas as "rumours",' he said.

'See, I told you the bond that we have with the president is deep. The media and the DA will try its best to create a rift between us, but he will stand by us like a rock. The president will defend us always,' he said, showing me the newspaper clippings.

I found the discussions of commercial issues of *The New Age* and ANN7 intriguing. There had been a lot of noise about *The New Age* and the way the government supported it, and it seemed to me that these discussions were probably around a similar kind of support for ANN7.

Nine

TAKING THE CHANNEL TO launch was full of challenges for me as the editor. We had to complete all hiring before the equipment started arriving and start training the staff and do test runs at least a month before launch.

I wanted a full month of dry runs on the integrated systems with the young team before I would be sufficiently confident to launch ANN7. But this seemed more impossible with every passing day.

The technical team only ordered the critical equipment in the middle of July 2013, and it looked like the delivery could be delayed until well after 9 August 2013, the launch date we had set.

Hiring was impeded by the fact that salaries were pegged at levels paid to journalists and technicians in India. It was very difficult to get senior South Africans at those budgets.

Moreover, many senior journalists who came for interviews told us they were apprehensive about working for a television station owned by the infamous Gupta family. They wanted written guarantees that they would not be made to toe the Gupta line on various issues in the newsroom. And, of course, Atul did not want to hire these candidates.

Getting credible presenters for the channel was proving to be a big headache. Nazeem contacted many presenters from rival channels, luring them with huge pay packages and flexible working hours. Not many took the bait.

The ones that did wanted double what was being offered because, in the words of one such presenter, she was 'bringing her credibility to the project'.

I was part of all of these meetings and saw first-hand the suspicion and doubt with which many journalists viewed Atul and his team. Most did not want to be part of a news station that would be, in their words, 'another *New Age*'.

Atul had a grand plan to overcome the issue with the dozen-odd presenters we needed. He revealed his plan in a review meeting in the last week of June 2013.

'I will ask Aslam to get the modelling agency to send us sexy young models who will present our bulletins. We will not have to deal with these ugly old bitches anymore. I will also get all the past Miss South Africas to come and present shows on our station,' Atul said as he pulled out his phone and dialled *New Age* creative head Aslam Kamal's number.

'Aslam, call Sheena and ask her to send 20 to 30 of her girls for an audition. We will not pay them anything right now, but they will have an opportunity to be on air if they are selected and will get a small stipend then. Get her to start tomorrow. Give them a small lunch… order a pizza lunch maybe for their effort from tomorrow.'

A model herself, Sheena Deepnarain ran an agency and, the way Atul spoke of Sheena, it sounded like they were old business associates.

I was baffled by this quick decision and execution.

'Models are not journalists. You surely don't think models will present news shows on your channel? It takes months of training and years of experience before you get a presenter ready for the prime shows,' I said with a sense of outrage.

'Look Rajesh, you are from India, you do not know the South African viewer. Have you seen *Russia Today*? People do not watch it because it has better news than Al Jazeera or CNN, they watch it because it has hot blondes presenting the news. It will work for us; you will see,' Atul shot back.

'I do not agree with you. We do not have time to train and experiment with 30 models. We need 10 sharp presenters who are journalists to start off with, and that is what we should be looking at. You cannot have greenhorns on prime time and I am clear about that,' I said firmly.

'Okay, we will get journalists for prime time, but we will have models for all the other bands, and that is final. I have taken a decision, and that is final,' Atul said, frowning, his voice raised.

I looked at Nazeem. He may not have agreed with the decision, but he kept mum.

Before this meeting Nazeem and I had agreed that we needed to up the salaries budget to bring on board five of the best television presenters in South Africa and quickly train five more from the lot of reporters we had hired or shortlisted.

We had planned to get a team of 10 young students to train with a meteorologist and producer from India to do the complicated weather bulletin.

The plan was also to have the sports, entertainment, Africa and business teams to produce and present their own bulletins. I had suggested the name of a top presenter from Europe to train the presenters and acquaint them with 'standard operating procedures' for technical glitches such as a failed teleprompter or play-out.

But all of that planning had been reduced to dust by Atul. His plan saved the company thousands of rands, but it cost the company millions in lost reputation, as we found out post-launch.

'Why do you want to hire a European to train the presenters? We will have a Miss South Africa train them. She has hosted hundreds of shows, and this would be a piece of cake for her. The viewers will have a bombshell every time they tune in to ANN7,' Atul said.

I was in despair, and there was little I could do as a professional manager.

Atul wanted Gerry Rantseli-Elsdon to train the models. Gerry was hired to present the breakfast show, which had been branded 'Vuka Africa'.

The show needed a lot of work and a team of researchers, producers and presenters. They had to work around the clock to produce the three-hour programme that was to air every morning from Monday to Friday.

Gerry had not even been hired yet, let alone the team, when Atul took the decision to ask her to train the models. He wanted each model to memorise a few lines and say those looking into the camera. A hired cameraman was asked to record these, burn them on a CD and send it to him for final approval.

He would select the models with whom he wanted to continue, these models would then be sent to Gerry for training.

Gerry was given a table and chair, a white board and a training room. Some days she had a camera at her disposal. She had no teleprompter, professional monitors or audio equipment in the initial weeks.

Gerry shortlisted and brought with her a bunch of models she thought could be trained to present. Nazeem and Atul also had a list of presenters sent by President Zuma. This included former government spokesperson Jimmy Manyi.

Jimmy failed miserably when he did his test interrogation with Atul on the Waterkloof issue. Nazeem, the top editorial team, me and Atul himself knew he was stiff on camera and reluctant to ask tough questions. But despite these shortcomings, he was hired.

'We have to hire him; President Zuma will have it no other way. But we do not have to put him on air until he is perfect. We will have someone train him,' Nazeem said after looking at the CD of the pilot he shot with Atul.

Jimmy resisted the idea of training and did not want the editorial team to assist him with research or even fixing guests.

The others recommended by President Zuma, including a radio show presenter who was the daughter of an African National Congress (ANC) leader, declined Nazeem's offer after coming to the office for several rounds of meetings and interviews.

Many recommended by President Zuma asked for a salary that was well out of the ANN7 salary band fixed by Laxmi.

'Just because they have been recommended to us by President Zuma, they think they can ask for exorbitant salaries. Some of them are not even worthy of being trainees here,' Nazeem told me after interviewing one such candidate.

The models who came to audition were confident young women who wanted to make a career in television news. They waited hours to be auditioned and trained, spending this time in small rooms before their turn came.

All of them were being exposed to television studios, news presentation, teleprompters and cues for the first time. Their lack of familiarity with the medium was evident on screen.

However, there was no dearth of young talented students from various media schools who wanted to join ANN7. Many of them had completed internship stints and were brimming with confidence and eagerness. Most of them had never worked with the technology we were proposing to bring in. Many had never worked in a television newsroom before in their lives. But it was encouraging that they were quick learners, and most had a knack for technology.

We had the first major batch of employees – mostly trainees – join the team on 1 July 2013. Besides the trainees, there were camera operators and video editors.

One senior appointment we made then was the immensely talented André Oosthuizen, a soft-spoken, patient, humble, technical genius with decades of experience in television post-production. He joined as head of the video editing team.

André's team was very young and inexperienced but eager to learn from him. André was affectionately called 'Daddy' by his team for the way he mentored them and nurtured their talent.

The studio was still far from complete and more of a hazardous, noisy, dusty construction site cluttered with scaffolding, construction workers and building material.

The initial team did not have a functioning newsroom or equipment.

Just a day before they started, 10 camera units purchased from Singapore had arrived, and the IT team had set up about a dozen low-end computer systems on networks loaded with home-video editing software for use until the ordered equipment arrived.

We had asked international news agencies Associated Press Television Network, Agence France Presse TV and Reuters to give us test video feeds, so we could evaluate services before we took a final decision on subscribing to one.

I was very keen for the team to start work from day one and get as much experience as possible before the launch.

The day started early with an editorial meeting. Some of the trainees were assigned to select international stories from the agency feeds. Trainees who came up with good ideas for local news stories would be sent out with a camera team.

The teams would come back, write their scripts and edit their video packages with André's team on the temporary low-end edit systems. Voice-overs were recorded on cameras in the newsroom.

The sound of the construction in the studio was always part of these recordings. This was a time when the construction work in the studio was at its noisiest… drills, hammers, falling pieces of plaster and wood. The acoustically treated voice-over booths were weeks away from completion.

The temporary servers and computers were too slow for the work that was being done and would crash often. Editing 10 new reports and putting together a half-hour bulletin on a slow home version editing system would take up to 16 hours.

It was frustrating working with unreliable systems. Young producers and reporters would finish editing a story in four hours only to realise that the system had crashed and their work was not recoverable.

But regardless of the difficulties and challenges we faced, we never failed to bring out a bulletin each day. André would spend hours first guiding the young editors and then painstakingly piecing together a bulletin. When I look back, I think not having too many experienced people on board was a blessing in disguise. Many professionals would have just refused to work under these conditions and walked out.

Never once did the young team, from all races and backgrounds, appear to feel daunted by the delays and major system flaws. They were always ready to go the extra mile, start again if their first attempt failed, and were always cheerful about learning new skills and techniques.

Many of the young people would come into the office by 7 am and leave only past midnight. This enthusiastic lot worked seven days a week.

Atul allowed the Indian staff to take office cars home after work and drive back in those cars in the morning, but he refused to allow the South African staff the same privilege.

He agreed to have two cars drop the local staff as a temporary measure after I protested against this discriminatory practice. This meant that dozens of young South African journalists who finished their work around midnight had to wait for a few more hours before the cars returned from the previous trip before getting dropped off.

I insisted that the management either get a larger vehicle or organise more cars to transport the staff. There was no public transport available at that time of the day. Some of the staff would get home at 3 am and were expected to get back to work by 7 am. This was clearly abusive.

One night, as I was preparing to leave the office at 1 am, I found about a dozen journalists waiting at reception for a vehicle to take them home. Some of them had been at the office since seven the previous morning and were expected back in six hours' time. I called up Uday and asked him to provide a car immediately to take them home.

'Atul ji has given strict instructions not to allow more than two cars for the local staff. Your car has been arranged. Why don't you go home? The car that has gone to drop staff in Pretoria will be back in an hour and will take them then,' Uday said.

I was disgusted.

'Uday, I will not leave the building until the last of the South African staff have left. This is inhumane treatment. I will sit on the floor in reception and will leave only when the last of my colleagues have left. I will do this every day until more cars are organised, do you understand?'

I had to do this for three days before transport for the South African staff was streamlined.

I was told Atul was not happy about my sit-in. But he did not confront me because this was the crucial pre-launch phase, and there were a lot of other things to worry about. He did address it later when I met him after a review meeting in his room though.

'The South Africans are a difficult lot. If you give them a lift back home they will seek it as a right. Even those in the morning shift will wait until the evening to make use of the free lift back home. These are leeches that want to suck the organisation dry,' he told me with a straight face.

'But now there are no shifts. Almost everyone is working from morning to midnight because we are on slow temporary systems. There is no public transport available when their work ends. We must provide a few more cars or a couple of buses to drop the staff until we get our professional equipment and work in shifts. Otherwise it will kill the kids,' I said.

'I will ask Sahara Computers to provide us with a bus. Don't bother yourself with these small issues,' he said.

The bus was never made available.

The dust and the noise from the construction site were adding to the stress levels. We were not offered any protection against the dust and paint fumes we were exposed to at that time.

Atul would shamelessly walk around the site wearing an elaborate mask. The fact that his employees were exposed for many more hours than him did not even seem to cross his mind.

A few protective masks were handed out after a couple of employees had to be rushed to hospital from the office with respiratory distress. But the masks were cheap and offered little protection.

The lack of a proper canteen was also a major problem, especially on the weekends, as restaurants and grocery stores nearby were either closed or had limited hours. This was a major issue, as the team did not have time to leave the office complex to eat.

Krishna was cooking free meals for the Indian staff and initially also for the builders who were staying at the site. Atul then reluctantly extended the meals to all Indian staff, saying this would be discontinued after the launch.

However, this benefit was never extended to the South African

Indentured

employees. It was extremely distressing to see the Indian staff sit down for dinner after a long day's work while the South Africans were not invited to join. Many of the South Africans had to go hungry, as there was no place nearby selling food that was open at that time.

The delay in the construction of the studio and operational area was something that led to more stress between the technical team and Atul, who would now openly abuse Y P Singh and berate the team almost every day.

'What the hell is Laxmi Goel doing sitting in India? His incompetent technical team is giving me high blood pressure here and ruining my health. He should come here and see for himself how lousy his technical team is,' Gupta said at a review meeting.

Atul would take a CD of the news bulletin produced during the day back home with him every evening.

He would come back with feedback from the family the next day.

It was mostly criticism from his youngest brother, Tony.

'Tony says the audio on the CD is very poor and the editing is not slick. He says we are nowhere near the quality of CNN or BBC,' Atul said after watching a CD one day.

He had very little understanding of television or the primitive conditions under which the bulletins were being produced.

He also did not believe in incentivising the hard work that the young team were putting in. All the employees officially had a 45-hour work week but were easily putting in over 70 hours without complaining.

Nazeem suggested offering a financial incentive to keep the morale of the young team high ahead of the launch.

'Nazeem, just organise some pizza and Coke for these people, and they will be over the moon. Food is all they really want. That is incentive enough. No need to pay them anything,' Atul said.

Things were chaotic in the newsroom but were set to get even worse as we got closer to the launch date. Critical pieces of equipment were still missing, and there was never going to be enough time to fix bugs in the system after these were integrated with the main server. Adding to the chaos would be the nearly two dozen new journalists and technicians Laxmi proposed to bring from India. Most of them had worked only on established news channels and had no experience of trouble shooting in a new set-up that had not yet stabilised.

Ten

THE SECOND MEETING with President Zuma happened in July.

'He feels good if we give him the feeling that he is moulding the news station. It is always good to have the head of state on your side. He will give us some suggestions. We do not have to follow all his suggestions, but we will make polite noises and we will follow the suggestions that are acceptable to us,' Atul told me before the meeting, reiterating a point his brother and he had made many times before.

Like the previous one, this meeting took place on a Sunday morning. Ashu Chawla came in his car to pick us up from the Midrand office. He was mostly silent during the ride to President Zuma's residence in Pretoria. He seemed preoccupied and kept checking his phone for messages as he drove.

'Have you lived here for long, Mr Chawla?' Arun asked him.

'Yes, 17 years. I have been with Atul ji right through at Sahara Computers,' he said with a rare smile through his moustache.

Indentured

'So you are a regular South African then?' Arun asked.

'Yes,' Ashu replied, curtly.

He then played a CD with raunchy Hindi Bollywood songs referred to in India as 'item numbers'.

'So you have a taste for "item numbers", Mr Chawla. Now that's a facet of your personality that we never knew about,' Arun teased Ashu.

He smiled sheepishly and continued driving. Arun had run out of topics to strike up a conversation, and Ashu was silent throughout the remainder of the journey.

As we reached the security gate at the president's residence, the security guards recognised him and waved the car in.

We went to the same room we had been waiting in the last time and sat in exactly the same places.

Ashu went to check on the president's availability.

Nazeem, Moegsien, Atul and Ajay arrived about half an hour later. Ashu sprang to his feet and touched the brothers' feet. The seating arrangement was identical to that of the last meeting.

'Rajesh, today I will ask President Zuma to give us a broad overview on editorial policy and also some suggestions on who we should hire as presenters. We will hear what he has to say, but we will only do what we think suits our vision,' Ajay Gupta told me.

As long as it was just a formality and we were not bound by what he was saying, I was happy to play the game they were playing with the president. I nodded.

The video logo montage or the 'channel ID' for ANN7 had been made by a graphics designer in India and had reached us just a few days before the meeting. Atul wanted me to load a copy on my laptop so we could show it to the president.

'Rajesh, we will show it to the president today. We can make a million presentations on paper, but he will know the project is progressing fast only when he sees videos. He is a simple man. I am sure he will be very happy to see it,' Atul said.

'Sir, the president has many visitors from his family today. I have sent a message that you have arrived, and he will join us very shortly,' Ashu told Ajay.

The president arrived shortly thereafter.

He was shown the channel ID. He asked to see it again and again.

'Sir, if you like this montage, we will give it the final go-ahead,' Atul said.

'It looks good. It is impressive,' President Zuma said, asking to see it one more time.

He had the copy of the presentation we had given him in the last meeting with him.

'I have a few suggestions. We must not convert this into a publicity channel for the ANC and me. If we do that, we will have no credibility. You must present the views of the opposition and my rivals in the ANC as well. The push in our favour should be subtle. You are a seasoned journalist. You know how that can be done… eNCA only presents the government and me negatively. We need a channel that presents the positives that the government is doing,' Zuma said looking at me.

Despite Atul's constant reminders that we'd only do what 'suits our vision', President Zuma's directives on editorial policy puzzled me.

'I will be in Mpumalanga next week, and I will meet people in the local communities and announce measures for their welfare. But I am sure eNCA will not cover that. Their reporter will seek out opposition supporters and do a negative story on how the locals hate me and feel I have done nothing for them,' Zuma said.

'Sir, we will have a reporter and camera operator attached to you at all times. You will have to ensure that they are accommodated in the plane that you travel on. We will do a live telecast of all your engagements. We have outside broadcast vans,' Ajay said, almost cutting in.

'Yes, that can be easily arranged. But your coverage will be shallow if you come with me. Our teams must move in two days ahead of me and do background reports that tell viewers how our policies are helping the people, so that they get the full picture and not the distorted one they get now. Is that possible?' Zuma asked.

'Sir, we will make it possible. We have the technology to go live from anywhere in the country, and we have bureaus in every province. We can send reporters with you, and we will also send reporters in advance. The positives of the government will surely be highlighted,' Ajay answered, with folded hands.

'If newspapers and television news channels show that the people are happy and benefitting from what the government is doing for them, the people will believe it. What is happening now is just the opposite. Show the critics saying that the government is not working, but also show many cases of how the government is changing lives. That way we keep the credibility and we also show the government in a positive light,' Zuma said.

'I am sure you will have the best international standards of production. That is very important. The news bulletins should be slick,' he added.

Nazeem then asked him to recommend journalists and presenters.

It was at this meeting that Jimmy Manyi's name first came up. 'He will be most suited for your talk shows. If you want, I will speak with him as well,' Zuma offered.

'I am sure there are many presenters available. Just do let me know if there is any high profile journalist you may have selected,' he added.

The conversation was now beginning to sound like an internal HR meeting. He had allocated two hours of his time on a Sunday, while his family was waiting, to ANN7. The intensity of his interest in the project was like that of a full shareholder.

President Zuma was happy to sit for hours getting briefed and giving input on minute aspects of the venture. The time he spent helping out with the 'commercial' aspects was most intriguing.

'Sir, the DA has a very effective PR machinery, and they churn out press releases very day, twisting facts and turning them against the government. Most journalists earn a salary by just reproducing DA press releases and news reports. We have to keep such journalists out.' Nazeem said this to immediate nods from President Zuma and the Gupta brothers.

I exited the second meeting the same way I did the first. Ajay asked the TV team to leave, so that the newspaper team could have some alone time with the president.

I later asked Nazeem why President Zuma insisted on lecturing us on editorial and personnel matters.

'Don't you know? Hasn't Laxmi ji told you already? He has a big say in this venture. His son Duduzane holds 30 per cent in the company. His involvement is very critical for the first year of our operations. If we are able to get government advertisements, we will be able to break even in the first year,' he told me.

If this were true, it would explain a lot, and it felt as though everything was falling into place.

The news channel I was heading would be a pro-ANC, pro-Zuma channel that was promoted and run by not only people close to President Zuma but by President Zuma himself. If Nazeem had his facts straight and Zuma held the shares through his son, he would be projected positively in the news bulletins.

In this scenario I could see how he would use his position as president to ensure government advertising for the station.

It also seemed, if this was the truth, that there was a clear conflict of interest as his son had a stake in not just the Gupta-owned newspaper but also the proposed television news channel.

Indentured

As a 30 per cent stakeholder, his son would get 30 per cent of the profits earned from the revenues the president was helping them generate.

Eleven

By 10 July, Shantanu Chatterjee, the output head, Umesh Vohra, the input head, and all the Indian professionals I had hired in Delhi had arrived and dived straight into the launch process.

Most of those we had hired were gems who took to the work like fish to water. Zaida Gangat, Comfort Tshabalala, Tsunag Lefafa, Lindokuhle Mnisi, Ramaupi Arnold Makgoo, to name a few, worked night and day to make sure that the bulletins were not just produced every day but improved constantly.

With years of experience working with top networks in South Africa and abroad between them, Caroline Samuels, Peter Stemmet, Mahreen Chenia and Benjamin Leshoro made a great sports desk.

Nausheena Mahomed joined the business desk as a reporter/presenter.

With these additions the bulletin was starting to have diverse content and distinct segments: political, sports, business and international news. A small team was also putting together an

Africa bulletin. Umesh worked hard to bring together a network of international reporters and stringers who were starting to send in content as well.

All the newsgathering cameras had come in by now, and the reporting teams were out covering the major news stories in Gauteng province.

However, we still had dozens of vacancies on the output desk: experienced people who could sub-edit television scripts, run-down producers who could work shifts building bulletin structures, and panel producers who could put bulletins together in the PCR.

I was asked to take over the hiring of PCR staff from Y P.

The PCR was still weeks away from being fully operational, but we needed the staff to start working as soon as it was ready. I found three South Africans who could have been hired immediately as the head of PCR and recommended one to Laxmi and Atul. But the salary he was drawing at the time was three times the budget Laxmi had fixed for the position. And he wanted 10 per cent more than his existing salary.

We had also not found a single local person who would join the master control room, or MCR.

'We will get the full PCR and MCR team from India. It will be much cheaper, and also they will work around the clock. Atul tells me the locals want five-day weeks and eight-hour shifts and many expensive benefits. I want the broadcast van staff and engineers from India as well,' Laxmi told me when I called him to discuss the issue.

'But we must hire South Africans, even if we hire trainees and bring in trainers. The young South Africans we have in the other departments are shaping up well, and no one knows the country like they do,' I protested.

But by then Laxmi and Atul had already decided to bring in dozens of Indian personnel. Laxmi wanted me to suggest some of my Indian contacts. I was against this but had to obey executive orders.

Sensing my reluctance to bring in more people from India, Laxmi asked me to get Shantanu to make a list of people who could be hired.

Since the launch date was imminent, these people needed to be in Midrand at the earliest.

Laxmi got his old confidant Sanjay Pandey, who worked as ANN7 production head, to headhunt cheap technical staff in New Delhi from the various Hindi and regional language channels in India. Some of the people he hired in haste did not speak English.

Ashu had told Atul during a meeting that 'Intra-company transfer visas for so many Indian employees would take at least a week and a half.' He said it was not wise to seek so many visas simultaneously, as it could bring the people involved in issuing these visas into question if there is a 'scrutiny in the future'.

'We can give them offer letters and ask them to apply for tourist or business visas. They will get these visas in a couple of days and can fly in immediately to help with the launch. It is illegal for them to work, but we will convert the visas into intra-company transfer visas in due course,' Ashu suggested.

'That is a good idea. If we don't like their work, we can ask them to leave when their tourist visas expire. We will get the proper work visas for only those who we think are good,' Atul said.

I was dead set against this arrangement, as I was convinced it violated the law and would require me to sign on the employment approval documents. Also it was unfair to ask people to come to South Africa promising them permanent positions and send them back two months later if Mr Gupta 'did not like their work'.

I registered my protest with Nazeem and told him that I was party to this arrangement under protest and that as editor it was not right on my part to go with the plan. He justified the decision as an 'executive decision' and the only option left as the launch date was just days away.

But this possibly illegal route was not the only option. They could have delayed the launch to a more reasonable date, or they could have hired qualified South Africans, some of whom were available to join immediately.

What worried me more was Laxmi's plan to pay the new employees a month's salary in cash in India without any tax deductions. Doing this is illegal in India.

Employee salaries are supposed to be credited into their accounts or through cheques or direct transfers after tax is deducted. This was being done to ensure that there was no evidence that these employees worked for ANN7.

This was not the only time Laxmi paid cash. The vendors who were commissioned to make the channel logo and video montage were also paid in cash.

The set designer and fabricator, the construction workers and others who came from India were also paid in cash, probably without tax being paid either in India or South Africa. The amount paid out in cash ran into millions of Indian rupees. I had warned Arun and Nazeem about this but was told there was no violation of South African laws here. I had serious doubts about this.

Meanwhile, the SABC announced that it would launch its much delayed 24-hour news channel on 1 August and that it had been offered the 404 slot by DStv.

I was told that the president's office had been approached to pressure DStv to offer the 405 slot to ANN7.

After initially insisting that they would not offer us the slot until they were satisfied with the technical and production standards over one month of test broadcasting, DStv suddenly gave in.

Even as ANN7 was offering three bulletins a day produced on primitive systems and equipment nowhere near the quality standards prescribed by DStv, it was announced internally that DStv had been 'pressured' through President Zuma's office to oust *Russia Today* from the 405 slot and give it to us.

The delay in the construction of the studio was creating further friction between Y P and Atul. Things came to such a point that not a day went by without them exchanging harsh words. Invariably Atul would end the conversation asking Y P to get out of the project and the country.

This led to further strain between the two shareholders, Atul and Laxmi.

The hiring of technical staff was still an area of major concern, mere days before the launch. This meant that there were not enough hands on deck to run even a single eight-hour shift.

I found Nazeem the most reasonable in management and given the circumstances told him that launching the channel on 9 August would be impossible.

But Nazeem was a newspaper man and did not know much about television. He spent many hours in meetings with me and the team from India, trying to understand the various technical aspects of launching a channel. He battled to plead our case.

And so Laxmi was summoned again.

'Laxmi Goel has left this stupid technical team here to traumatise me, and he himself is having fun in Delhi. Why should I take all the stress of launching the channel? He should bloody well come here and oversee the construction and installation himself. This Y P Singh is a disgrace. I will call Laxmi and ask him to take the next flight to South Africa and deal with this situation,' Atul roared after a review meeting.

The message was conveyed to Laxmi, and he called me that evening and said he would come to South Africa in a few days.

'Make arrangements for me to stay at a guest house. I may not want to stay with the Gupta family when I am there. Y P Singh is getting old now and is making a mess of things; he forgets things and sits on decisions. I have asked Ravi Puri and Sunil Kumar from my brother Jawahar's company to take the next flight and reach South Africa to take over from Y P. I am sure they will turn things around in a few days,' Laxmi assured me.

Ravi and Sunil were old confidants of Laxmi and were the people who had travelled to China and other parts of the world to order everything for the station, from the broadcast equipment to the office furniture. They had done all the negotiations with the vendors, including coordinating the vendor support training for the staff on various systems. They were employees of Jawahar's company Dish TV.

They arrived in Midrand a couple of days before Laxmi Goel.

'It is impossible to launch by 9 August. I will tell Laxmi ji. A lot of work needs to be done,' Ravi told me when I met him on the day he arrived.

'Telling Laxmi Goel is not the problem. Try telling this to Atul Gupta. You should see the way he berates and scolds Y P Singh when he talks about possible delays,' I said.

Ravi assured me that he would ask Laxmi to seek more time for the launch from Atul. But we knew this would lead to a lot of conflict. And even if Atul agreed to a postponement, it would not be for more than a couple of weeks at best. It would take at least three months for a proper smooth launch.

At this point the team was working long hours and I was afraid they would burn out even before the launch. I hoped Atul saw reason. But I knew in my heart that he would never allow Laxmi to delay the project by more than a couple of weeks – if at all.

Twelve

THE THIRD MEETING WITH the president happened a few weeks later, in the first week of August. We had started producing news using a very basic PCR that was not fully integrated with the newsroom systems and the servers.

We were days away from our amended launch date of 21 August, and the technical team was nowhere close to handing over the studio or a smoothly functioning PCR or even integrated video editing systems to the editorial team.

I was in the PCR overseeing the rolling of a bulletin when Atul sent word that I must meet him at the cafeteria immediately.

'We have an appointment with President Zuma this evening. He wants a quick review of the project, and I would like you to take the bulletins we have produced over the last few days. We have to make him happy, so make sure we take bulletins where a majority of the stories show him in a good light. I do not want a bulletin filled with Malema,' he said.

Indentured

Former Zuma loyalist Julius Malema had just founded a new opposition party to the ruling ANC called the Economic Freedom Fighters.

The bulletins we had produced at that time were, unsurprisingly, full of technical glitches and were anchored by a group of models hired by Atul and trained by Gerry Rantseli-Elsdon. The young women were very raw, clueless about the news they were reading and very unfamiliar with a studio setting.

I was not comfortable showing these bulletins to anyone outside of the newsroom. They were produced as practice or dry runs, nothing more.

The plan was to take a chip reader to President Zuma's Pretoria house and connect it to a monitor for him to see the bulletins. I went back to the PCR and asked the team to put a few of the bulletins we had produced on a chip. The team put four recent bulletins on the chip and handed it to me.

We left in Atul's car at about 7 pm. Ashu and Ajay were going to meet us there.

Nazeem travelled with me in Atul's chauffeur-driven car.

'Has someone informed Arun?' I asked Nazeem.

'Don't bother with Arun. He is not going to this meeting,' Nazeem replied.

Moegsien was in Cape Town and was unable to join us.

'We must discuss the IEC issue with him today. I am told the IEC is set to run a major advertising campaign in all the big newspapers. It is unfair for them not to advertise in *The New Age*,' Nazeem told Atul.

'Ajay bhai has already briefed him about this. We will get some action today,' Atul replied.

Atul had organised a chip reader and a 14-inch broadcast-quality monitor to be sent to Ashu earlier in the day. He was to bring these for the meeting. We were ushered into the same waiting room where we had been before.

Soon Duduzane Zuma walked in and greeted us before proceeding to hug the Gupta brothers.

'We have a surprise for you today, Dudu. We will show you the bulletins we have been producing,' Ajay Gupta said with an animated movement of his hands.

'Good, so we should move to the next room. It has a large TV.' He started moving out, and all of us followed him.

This was a much larger living room that had various seating arrangements and a large TV set. We sat around a coffee table. Ashu took out the chip reader and the cables. There was not enough cable to connect the chip reader to the large TV mounted on one of the walls. I gave the chips to Ashu. He placed the chip reader and the monitor he brought with him on a coffee table and connected the cables.

President Zuma walked into the room and wanted to know about the equipment.

'We want to show you a few bulletins that we have produced,' Duduzane said.

This was the first time Duduzane was seeing the bulletins. He had no clue about the process and effort that had gone into producing these. He had never attended a single meeting or even bothered to visit the studio and learn about the problems there, but today in front of his father he had no qualms about taking credit for the bulletins.

The Gupta brothers smiled indulgently as he spoke.

'Sir, we want feedback on this too. We want you to tell us if we are on the right track. Our equipment is not fully here, and this is not 100 per cent of what we will look like when we launch. This is maybe 50 per cent,' Ajay said with a broad smile on this face.

Ashu pressed the play button, and the first bulletin started with the channel ID followed by the headlines. The anchor made a few fumbles, but that did not seem to bother the president. He watched the first 15 minutes with rapt attention.

'Sir, we can fast forward the bulletin, so that you can see the others too,' Ajay offered.

'Let it go on, I want to see some more,' President Zuma said.

'Daddy likes the anchor, his eyes light up every time she comes on. Is that why you want to see some more?' Duduzane joked.

Everyone in the room broke into laughter.

'See the visuals we are using for Malema? It is of him getting out of a helicopter. He looks corrupt, does he not? We always use these visuals when we talk about Malema. This is a subtle way of telling the people he is corrupt without saying a word,' Ajay said, pointing to the screen.

President Zuma smiled.

Ajay knew nothing about the content. The editorial team used these visuals because these were the only visuals available in the archives bought from the SABC. He had just made that up to please the president and from the look on his face it seemed he was happy.

President Zuma watched all the bulletins.

'You have a good thing on your hands. This is much better than the bulletins on the SABC. Those are horrible. I like the way you have used the graphics. It reminds me of the international channels. If this is what you will look like on launch day you will be a hit,' President Zuma said with a smile.

The SABC had launched its 24/7 news channel a few days before, on 1 August 2013.

This was the endorsement the Gupta brothers were looking for. They had softened President Zuma before their meeting on commercials, and they could hardly hide their glee.

'So you say the final product will be much better than this?' President Zuma asked, looking at me.

'Sir, it will surely be much better, as we will have completed the integration by then and will have much more equipment at our disposal to make the bulletins slicker. I am not very happy with these bulletins; they are just practice runs,' I replied.

'I am happy with even this. You guys keep this up.' President Zuma was beaming.

'Sir, you must come and press the button to inaugurate the channel on the 21st. I know you have declined before, but you must inaugurate the channel. We will have our editors do an exclusive interview with you at the venue,' Atul said with a broad smile and his hands folded.

'That will not send the right message. It will not do your credibility any good. I am part of the project, and I am always ready to give an interview after a few weeks,' Zuma replied firmly.

At this point Ajay asked me to go back to the office while Atul, Nazeem and Duduzane met him for discussions about the newspaper and commercial issues.

I was told the next day by Nazeem and Atul that they had secured 20 million rand's worth of business the previous evening.

By this time, I had decided to resign as editor at ANN7 and go back to India after the launch. It was happening without the extensive training I had suggested. It was happening without test runs with all systems and equipment in place.

But what really pushed me to resign was the violation of editorial integrity and the dubious commercial dealings that I had seen with my own eyes.

Thirteen

MY OPPOSITION TO THE plan to recruit more Indian staff on illegal visas with no job guarantee and exploitative working conditions was not taken kindly by Laxmi. He began recruiting without consulting me and involved Indian journalist Vishnu Shankar to conduct interviews in Delhi, along with Sanjay Pandey, who worked as ANN7 overall production head.

I did not agree with many of the people Laxmi hired. Most of them had qualifications and experience that were easily available in South Africa. We had identified South Africans who were suited for those positions, but they were not being hired because they were more expensive and would want to work as per South African labour laws. Many of the people hired from India were very young and were working for second-rate Hindi-language news channels.

Atul would declare grandly in meetings that this project would train and empower young South Africans, especially black people, and give them international-standard television production skills.

Indentured

But what was happening now was totally different. Dozens of young Indians were being brought in on tourist and business visas to take South African jobs.

Adding to the stress at this time were rumours circulating in India that Vishnu would take over as the output editor from Shantanu at ANN7 very shortly. Some of the candidates interviewed by Vishnu called Shantanu and me to tell us that Vishnu introduced himself as the output head at ANN7.

I confronted Atul with this news.

'Laxmi ji wanted Vishnu to come and train the staff here, but I do not know if he has hired him as the output head,' he said.

'Shantanu Chatterjee quit his job at a top Indian news station to come here and join ANN7 as output head; how can Laxmi ji get someone else in as the output head? Also, don't you think I should be consulted on something as critical as training?' I was angry now.

'Look, I do not know what this Shantanu does all day. He sits on his chair peering into the computer and does not move an inch. How do I know if he is working or watching Sex.com? And as far as the training is concerned, it is a proposal that Laxmi ji has mooted; we have not taken a decision on that,' Atul said.

'Shantanu holds a key position. If he were not working, you would not see the bulletins that you see every day,' I told him.

Atul did not understand much about the operations of a television newsroom, and his blunt statements made my resolve of quitting after the launch only stronger.

I told him that we were at a very critical stage ahead of the launch, and any decision on training needed to be taken with a lot of thought and consultation. He dismissed the suggestion. He clearly did not know what I was talking about.

Laxmi arrived at O R Tambo airport and was received by Arun Aggarwal. Ajay's bodyguards went inside the airport to receive him.

He met Arun and told him he would come to the office shortly. He got into a car from the Gupta fleet and left for the Gupta residence at Saxonwold.

Within minutes he called Arun and asked him to pick him up from the highway a few miles from the airport. He had had a very bitter phone conversation with Atul and had decided not to be a guest at the Gupta residence. But before Arun could reach the designated point to pick Laxmi up, Tony had convinced him to stay at the Gupta residence.

The situation was very tense. The launch was just days away.

However, Atul had not made the launch date public. He had plans to have a grand event 'rivalling the Gupta wedding' to launch ANN7, but the technological delays were driving him crazy and, in turn, he was driving the technology team crazy.

Laxmi came to the studio that afternoon. Atul made a point to leave the office for an 'urgent meeting' when Laxmi arrived.

My relations with him were strained because of his decision not to consult me about fresh hirings in India. He had also hired Sanjay and Vishnu without consulting me.

'Rajesh, Shantanu is a fool if he thinks there is a threat to his job. Vishnu is being brought here only to train staff on the output desk. If he is telling people that he will be the new output editor, then he is lying. And it is stupid for an editor to be worried about such small issues,' he said in a raised voice.

'As editor, we are engaged in training the team as well as bringing out a bulletin, without even the basic infrastructure in place. I raised the issue with you because Shantanu and I have been contacted by many journalists about what Vishnu has been telling them. It is not a small issue. The hushed manner in which the training and fresh hiring in India has been handled is impacting the morale of the core editorial team,' I replied.

'What do you want me to do? I have already paid Vishnu to train the staff for two months. If I cancel with him now, I will lose the money. Do you want me to do that?' he shot back at me angrily.

'I will go with what you have decided, but training is a key ingredient in a launch, and the editorial core team and I should have been consulted on the issue. I firmly believe Vishnu is not the best person suited for our requirements,' I said.

Laxmi clearly did not like what I said.

He then went on a tour of the studio site. He was not very happy with the progress. He realised there was no way the channel could be launched as planned. At this point, we were still working toward a 9 August launch date.

'We have to postpone the launch,' he told Y P and Ravi Puri.

'Sir, we must postpone the launch, but Atul Gupta will be very angry, he has been after our lives to launch on the ninth. He screams abuses at us if we even suggest the launch must be delayed by a few days. You must break the news to him and seek a fresh launch date after taking into account the time it will take for us to get the systems up and running. I have tried to explain things to Atul Gupta, but he is just not willing to see reason,' Y P told Laxmi.

I told Laxmi that it would be unfair to expect a world-class launch from a young team without giving them enough time to work on the systems after they have been installed and at least a month of practice on the new systems.

'It takes at least a month to train the staff and eliminate bugs and user errors on the system. You must put your foot down. Atul Gupta does not know what it takes to launch a channel, and he will only force us to have a half-baked, ill-prepared launch. We will be the laughing stock of the world if we do that. I will insist even now that we get world-class trainers to train our presenters and journalists,' I told Laxmi.

He was due to go for a meeting with the Gupta family in a few hours and was very stressed about what he would tell them. It was certain he would seek a postponement, but I was afraid he would be bullied into accepting a date that would leave the team with very little time to prepare.

Laxmi drove back with Atul after the meeting and called a meeting for the core team to fix the next launch date. The meeting was tense. Nazeem, the entire technical team and the core editorial team were there.

Laxmi announced with a grim face that there would be a delay in the launch of the channel. He asked me to suggest an alternate date. I told him again that the editorial team needed at least a month of practice runs on the installed and integrated systems before we could even talk about a launch date.

'We can't wait that long. We have to fix a date. Mr Singh will not even tell us when all the systems will be in place. We cannot wait for all systems to be in place before we start. We must fix a date and then ensure everything is in place by then,' Atul replied.

Ravi then assured the group that all systems would be up and running within the next two weeks.

'Two weeks, okay, then let us give it one more week for practice. Can we launch on the 21st?' Laxmi looked at the team. Y P nodded.

He looked at me next. He knew I would want a more detailed discussion on the realistic equipment delivery and installation schedules, vendor training and a longer training period before I would agree to a date. He told me bluntly then that 21 August would be the launch date regardless of what anybody thought.

My heart sank; this was clearly a disaster.

But I had to keep the newsroom morale high, so did not allow my doubts and scepticism to impede the work.

We continued with our routine of daily news meetings, production and reviews. The news packages produced by the young journalists were played out to the whole team every evening, and there was a session of critiquing. The senior team would spend an hour and a half giving feedback on ways to improve the editorial and production quality.

The young team learnt a lot from these sessions; the quality of the content improved with each passing day. What started off as amateurish student productions evolved slowly to news packages that we would be confident about putting on air.

There were worrying aspects about these sessions, though. Nazeem would chide reporters who did stories about issues raised by the DA and its leaders and asked them to focus instead on the 'real issues'. Atul would nod in agreement whenever he attended these sessions.

'The DA will issue a press release whenever puppies are born. Will we do stories about these puppies? These puppies are not the real issues. Focus on the positive stories,' Nazeem said at one of the review meetings.

By positive stories he meant stories that were positive to President Zuma and the government.

Stories about the launch of new political parties that were opposed to the ANC were also given a spin at one of the meetings.

Atul wanted the team not to focus on the agenda and plans of these parties and their leaders but to write them off as parties that mushroom ahead of the elections, headed by 'opportunistic' leaders. He argued that these parties would die either before the elections or after they are 'shown the door by the people' by getting few votes.

I asked the team to do balanced stories that showed all aspects and points of view in a story. But the message from Nazeem and Atul was clear. By the last week of July the video edit bay was finally made available to the team. None of the video editors had been trained on the Velocity system; they had worked primarily on the more widely used Final Cut Pro.

I was told that there would be no training on Velocity, as this had not been negotiated with the vendor.

For video editing head André Oosthuizen and his young team, this was a huge challenge. But to their credit they taught themselves the system in no time. They were able to edit all packages and put together a bulletin the same day they moved into the new video edit bay, despite the dust, fumes and noise coming from the construction site around them.

A virtual studio with green walls was set up and connected to the rudimentary PCR that was set up in the first week of August. Critical connections like the play-out, newsroom automation system and graphics were missing. Just beginning the roll of each bulletin would take hours.

The PCR did have a state-of-the-art audio system and video mixer, but there was no one to operate them. Input head Umesh Vohra volunteered to be the studio director, and André offered to take charge of the video switching. A young sound technician, Warren Naidoo, managed the audio panel. He had never worked on the system before but was determined to master it. He would come in a couple of hours before his shift and sit down with the user manual and try and figure out the knobs and faders. He stayed on afterwards to study the system even more. At that time, he would come into work at 5 am and leave well past midnight. His passion and energy were an inspiration for others on the team.

Shantanu had his hands full working on the bulletins and clearing the scripts that the young reporters and producers brought in. The output team was growing every day with a few young journalists joining each week, but the numbers were still inadequate, especially of experienced desk hands. He needed dozens more copy editors and panel and package producers – and soon.

But the shareholders' firm stand on not hiking salary budgets to get experienced journalists was a big impediment in filling these slots. The Indian nationals Laxmi wanted were still days away from reaching South Africa.

Our biggest worry at that time was the missing newsroom automation system. This was the system on which the reporters wrote their scripts and accessed the international news agencies. It also generated unique identification codes for each input and ensured that the right news story played in the right order. It was to be integrated with the main server and was the heart of editorial operations. We were going with the Associated Press' Electronic News Production System (ENPS) as our automation solution.

In all the other news channels that I had been a part of, training on the system was considered to be the most critical. It usually took up to five weeks to train 150 people on the various aspects.

User mistakes took days of constant training to correct and there were issues related to the compatibility with the server, and other broadcast processes and systems that cropped up from time to time.

Almost none of the people at ANN7 had ever worked on ENPS. Some had worked on similar systems, like Octopus or iNews, the more widely used newsroom automation systems. Most had never worked on a newsroom automation system at all.

I was told by Ravi that the ENPS contract involved training just a handful of people on the system. These employees were then required to train their colleagues.

This was disastrous for us, as the most senior editorial staff would have to focus first on getting trained and then training over 100 colleagues, at a time when we were required to focus 100 per cent on content.

So while the team had to work long hours to produce the bulletin on systems that were not completely installed and integrated, they also had to master the newsroom automation system.

I called this the zombie phase of the launch, as most of us where working over 16 hours a day on systems that kept failing; there was training and also reviewing and critiquing. This happened seven days a week.

The weekend programming was a serious headache, as the schedule depended a great deal on long-format programmes.

These needed to be produced in-house, as we could not afford independent outside producers.

Finally we brought in Mary Naidu, a talented and experienced expert on long-format programming.

Her job came with a set of complex conditions. She had to work on a shoestring budget; she had to use the news studios for the programmes and the studio where she was supposed to film and can episodes was still under construction.

To Mary's credit she quickly got a team together and started working on the 10 shows expected of her. This included two shows hosted by Arthur Mafokate on music and sport.

Mary's vast experience shone through as she improvised and used props and lighting to give the newsroom sets a distinct look and feel for each show. Faced with a steep bureaucratic process for issuing cash advances and seeking reimbursement, Mary would often buy props from her own pocket. She was reluctant to seek reimbursements, as she found the process too humiliating.

A café was created on the mezzanine floor with a glass wall, overlooking the studio and production area beyond. Atul made a habit of sitting here from morning to evening keeping a keen eye on every move in the area below.

He kept tabs on little things like how many times you took a break, how long you sat on your seat and how much time you spent talking to your colleagues. He would then confront me with the statistics.

'Did you know that X and Y take 10 cigarette breaks in a day?' or 'X was missing from his seat for three hours today, I don't know if you're keeping tabs on her work' and 'Y is always on the phone, and I am sure it is not all official calls. Are you keeping tabs?'

I found this most bizarre. I had worked in some fairly large television stations and had never seen shareholders keeping tabs on journalists in such a fashion. He would ask the HR team to give him timesheets daily and studied data on how much time each employee spent in the various areas of the building or when they came in or logged out.

He would be joined by Laxmi when he was in the country. And the two would sip endless cups of tea as they peered though the glass wall.

'Rajesh, you are not keeping an eye on that boy from graphics; he spent half an hour chatting with the models today. He saw me sitting here and he was still chatting away loudly with them. And the shameless girls were laughing and shouting loudly. Don't they know who I am? He was wasting their time and his; you must talk to him and the models and tell them not to talk to each other in the future. They should just eat quickly and quietly and get back to work,' Laxmi told me one day.

I was speechless. I explained to him that most of the employees worked well beyond their duty hours and were entitled to a few minutes of fun and laughter. Laxmi said nothing. He wanted the staff to know that they were constantly being watched and wanted them to work like slaves.

There was no way I would convey what Atul or Laxmi told me to the young team. I thought it was petty for the owners of the channel to sit like this and micromanage and nit-pick.

Atul was known to keep close tabs on the employees at *The New Age*, but there was no way I would allow him to do the same at ANN7 while I was editor.

Meanwhile, Atul got the *New Age* marketing manager, a young Indian national called Haranath Ghosh, to draft a press release announcing the launch of ANN7 on 21 August 2013.

Chantal Rutter Dros was named as the prime time presenter. Chantal had been persuaded by Nazeem to join. She had been assured a free hand in choosing the editorial content for her shows. She had, however, not been told about the state of readiness for launch.

She was taken to the PCR to see a bulletin rolling by Nazeem and me the day she joined. She was taken aback by the incomplete systems and the backbreaking work that went into producing a bulletin without automated systems.

Her own shows, as designed by me, had complicated formats that required perfect synchronisation between the PCR and the studio crew. But at the time she joined, with just days to go before the launch, critical elements had either not arrived or had not been assembled or placed on the set.

Chantal was nervous, like any professional in her position would be. She wanted Nazeem to postpone the launch until such time all systems were in place and the teams were trained. But Atul had already sent out a press release announcing the launch date, and there was no way he would allow it to be postponed again.

The advertising campaign announcing the launch was another disaster waiting to happen. Atul delayed giving the brief to a professional agency until only three weeks before launch. After initially saying that there would be a multimillion-rand-wattage publicity blitz, he cut down the campaign to mostly billboards in Gauteng and Cape Town.

'I do not trust the large white-owned agencies; they can very easily sabotage the whole thing. They are in bed with business interests inimical to us, and we can't trust the smaller agencies. So we will design and execute the whole campaign in-house; Ghosh will write the material with help from Rajesh, and he will also book billboards. Aslam will design the material,' Atul announced at a meeting he had called to discuss the campaign.

Haranath was involved in coordinating guests and organising *The New Age* Business Briefing. He was also the man behind the

Indentured

newspaper's rather uninspiring campaigns. He was not very happy being given more work.

'What should be the main themes in the campaign?' he asked me.

I told him to focus on the positives, on the things that differentiated us from our rivals. Like that we had a very young team, from all races. The emphasis on sports, business and entertainment, our unique set design that could allow us to give a distinct look to each bulletin and, of course, the new technology that would allow us to be faster and more efficient.

Atul rejected the first set of ideas Haranath came up with.

'I want bang for my buck. Make the material provocative, make it compelling enough for people to look at it and take direct digs at eNCA. Otherwise this campaign will come and go, and no one will ever notice it,' he told Haranath.

I was always wary of taking on the competition head-on through an ill-conceived advertisement campaign. The existing news channels had compelling content, and we had to have a proven track record before we took an aggressive approach to promoting ANN7.

Haranath wrote copy for about a dozen billboard designs and sent them to me for approval. I had very little time to look at them. I corrected grammar mistakes and sent them back to him.

Raman Bhatia from the ANN7 graphics team was asked to manipulate photographs from the internet and execute the designs made by *New Age* creative head Aslam Kamal. The result was a kitschy attention-seeking campaign that was low on quality and political correctness. Many of these billboards were the butt of jokes on social media and were removed following protests. This included one that read 'We are not old farts...'

Atul also put together a team to work out a grand programme for the launch function. He had made Haranath head this team as well. It had been decided earlier that the India team that was brought in to help launch the station would not be present at the event. Atul was afraid the station would then be branded as an Indian channel. He asked Haranath to showcase all the South African presenters and mix it up with a lot of 'song and dance'.

Laxmi asked me to make a speech at the event. I told him clearly that I would rather be with the team in the studio. I knew they would struggle, as much of the critical equipment would be fitted only on the day of the launch.

The technicians came to fit the jib four days before the launch and took the next two days to assemble it. At the same time the video walls were being fitted and operationalised.

The wireless audio communication system between the studio and the PCR had been unstable and would fail many times during a bulletin. This had not been rectified by the day of the launch.

About 15 days before the launch a core team of 15 senior editorial personnel were trained on ENPS. The technical team then connected all the computers in the newsroom and PCR with ENPS. A majority of the team were not yet proficient in ENPS by the day of the launch. Laxmi had hired an ENPS support technician from India, but she was clearly overwhelmed with the sheer number of people she was required to assist.

The technical team had connected the main server with ENPS, the graphics system, the teleprompter, video edit bays and the play-out system, but they had not fixed the bugs that would crop up from time to time.

Even a day before launch, bulletins would be disrupted as the server crashed or the play-out system would fail or the teleprompter would go blank on the presenters.

There was an experienced South African who could head PCR operations. He had worked for many years on the video switcher and other equipment ANN7 had and had experience as a studio director for top international sports networks. But Laxmi and Atul had decided not to hire him. Laxmi had hired a PCR head in India and he was to join a week before launch.

The situation in the run up to the launch was extremely stressful for the whole team, with new equipment being fitted, systems collapsing and new people from India coming and joining the team at the very last minute.

Vishnu, Sanjay and about two dozen Indian staff members arrived about a week before the launch. They were put up at various hotels and guest houses. Many of them did not speak English and had a tough time communicating and understanding the systems. Almost all of them came on visas that did not permit them to be employed in South Africa.

Laxmi had invited a huge delegation from India to attend the launch function. This included his extended family and associates.

The sports team led by Caroline Samuels, the Africa team and the team making the other bulletins through the day were going the extra mile to ensure the few days post-launch ran flawlessly, but the bugs in the system threatened to undo all the hard work.

Adding to the stressful environment was the constant scrutiny Atul and Laxmi subjected the team to, perched on the mezzanine floor behind the glass wall. They invited dozens of members from their extended families to come and visit the studio. They would come and sit in the newsroom and PCR looking at the team working as if they were at a circus. Pointing at people and talking loudly among themselves.

I was asked to assign Vishnu to a role on the output desk in the newsroom. When I asked Laxmi if he had the required visa to work in South Africa, he angrily asked me to do as I was told instead of asking questions.

Almost all of the Indian nationals working at ANN7 were paid their first month's salary in advance in 1 000 Indian rupee notes in India. Vishnu had brought two young sub-editors/producers with him.

Atul had his cronies Aslam and Saurabh Aggarwal keep tabs on the new arrivals as well. He got detailed reports on each of the employees and would openly discuss issues that he did not like about their behaviour.

'I heard that some of the new arrivals drink alcohol every night in the guest house. I want this to stop. If they drink so late into the night, they will never be able to give their 100 per cent in the morning. Please tell everyone that no one should drink alcoholic beverages until one month after launch. I will send them back to India if I hear that they have been drinking again,' he told me.

The focus of his attention was a particular young woman. He took objection to the clothes she wore and her social life.

'Aslam tells me that this woman does not go back to the hotel room we have booked for her. She goes in a car with a white guy and comes back with him in the morning. And she wears revealing clothes. We cannot allow this. I have asked Uday to check her out of the hotel room and send her to one of the guest houses. There is no way we will allow her to stay here after her tourist visa expires. To top it all she smokes. She is a girl. How can she smoke?' he asked me from his perch on the mezzanine floor one day, pointing at her.

These comments filled me with rage; I would never agree to tell anyone, let alone a young journalist, how to live her life or what clothes to wear. This was ridiculous.

Even more shocking was the fact that Atul seemed to have accessed her personal email. He knew, for instance, that she had not resigned from her last job and that she had come to South Africa on leave. He told me we knew this from her personal emails to friends.

I was appalled at how Atul as a shareholder in the company was targeting this young woman and at the surveillance of all staff in general.

Fourteen

My last meeting with President Zuma happened just 48 hours before ANN7 launched.

I was told that the president would make a quick trip to the studio to take a look for himself, and he was expected to stay on to see the rolling of a news bulletin. I was part of the team that would show him around.

This was a critical time as I was virtually camping in the office, sleeping for a few hours in a temporary rest area created for a few members of the core team on the first floor of the *New Age* office.

I was in the morning editorial meeting when I got a call from Aslam to come and receive the president.

'He is expected anytime now; Laxmi and Atul ji want you here immediately,' Aslam said.

Outside, I found Nazeem, Laxmi and Atul were already there. With them was Duduzane Zuma. I greeted them and waited with them for the presidential convoy to arrive.

It was cold that day and I had forgotten to take my jacket with me as I rushed out. Atul took the scarf he was wearing and wrapped it around my neck. I couldn't know at that time that this gesture would come back to haunt me later and subject me to humiliation and belittlement at the hands of the man who made it.

At that time, Karun Shawney, the head of production, sent a news camera team out to record the president's visit. The cameraman positioned himself to record the president getting out of his car. There were other crews he had set up inside the studio to record the president visiting various departments.

'We do not want any record of the president visiting the studio. Can you please ask the cameramen to go away. Also please tell everyone that there will be no recording of any of President Zuma's movements inside the studio… not even with cellphone cameras,' Atul whispered into my ear.

I called Karun and asked him to move the camera crews away. Atul wanted to keep the visit a secret, he was so suspicious and distrusting of everyone, but with over a 100 journalists in the studio, it was almost impossible.

The presidential convoy arrived and was taken to Laxmi's office.

'Sir, would you like to give an interview to our news team?' Atul asked. 'We will air it on launch day.'

'I have already said I will give ANN7 an interview later, after a few weeks. Any association with me at this time will be bad for the both of us,' President Zuma answered.

I led the team out of Laxmi's office, into the hall on the first floor where Mary Naidu and her programming team sat with the web team.

President Zuma played the part of a politician, going to each team member and shaking his or her hand. He waved to the employees who were not within hand-shaking reach.

We then took the stairs and moved into the newsroom. His

presence created a flutter on the floor. He waved to those working there. A live bulletin was being rolled at that time, and he waited for a while as the young anchor read her piece from the teleprompter.

He waved to her and moved into the corridor that housed the technical departments.

He first entered the PCR. Things were smooth in the PCR when he arrived. The systems were working fine. We had cut live to a reporter outside the courthouse where the Oscar Pistorius trial was happening.

He wanted to know from me what the exact function of each of the people in the PCR was. He also asked me about the audio panel, the vision mixer and outputs coming from various sources on the screens in front of him.

He stayed there for about 20 minutes. He then moved to the server room, the graphics room, the master control room and the video editing bay. He was shown a few of the promos produced by the team in the graphics room. He asked to see a few of the promos again.

On his way out he quickly slipped back into the PCR. This time there were technical glitches, the on-air graphics system collapsed, and the live sources started failing.

He stood at the PCR for another 15 minutes and then moved towards the door. Laxmi, Atul, Nazeem, Duduzane and I saw him off.

He said he was happy before he left. Atul assured him that the station would be run 'as per his guidance and wishes'.

Fifteen

TENSION WAS MOUNTING. The day of the launch was fast approaching and it was clear to me that we were not ready for it.

Formats for the flagship prime time show with presenter Chantal Rutter Dros and the morning band with Gerry Rantseli-Elsdon were finalised two days before the launch. Even then all the robotic studio cameras had not been operationalised. Chantal was nervous at first with the state of unpreparedness at which we were being forced to launch.

I told her we were like suicide bombers; we had no option but to execute the assignment given to us regardless of the huge challenges. I was amazed at her professionalism and dogged focus. It was tough for her; the Indian staff at the PCR gave her cues in a language and accent that was alien to her. It was frustrating for her, but that did not deter her. Even as the communications failed, or the teleprompter went blank, she soldiered on.

But the other presenters were not as experienced as Chantal and froze when the teleprompter went blank or their earpieces went silent during the practice runs ahead of the big day. The team knew it was not going to be perfect, but they decided they would strive to get as close to perfection as possible.

As per the plan the broadcast would cut live to the studio twice during the launch ceremony at the Sandton Convention Centre. Chantal was to present the bulletin on both these occasions. The stories that would feature in these bulletins and the guests who would feature in the discussions were finalised after the early morning meeting.

The day started early and by mid-morning family members of Atul and Laxmi arrived with the other invited guests from India to look at the 'circus'. They sat in the newsroom, literally staring at the news team. Another noisy lot of spectators sat in the PCR.

The launch ceremony was to be followed by regular programming, sports bulletins, the Africa and the late-night bulletin. The teams were in the office early and were working to ensure deadlines were met and their bulletins were produced and presented on time.

The first crossover to the studio was almost flawless. Chantal did a brilliant job, and all the packages and discussions went off smoothly. The jib movement and studio cameras were coordinated very well. As soon as the broadcast shifted back to the launch venue there was a thundering applause that rang through the newsroom with everyone congratulating each other with handshakes and hugs.

The second crossover was also well executed, but the last package could not play as the system malfunctioned. This was just the beginning of system errors that plagued us through the night.

Caroline Samuels and Mahreen Chenia from the sports desk were all set to host *Game On*, the prime time sports show, when at the last minute the teleprompter and the play-out failed. On live television the two young presenters waited for many awkward seconds for the studio director to cut into a break and play promos.

But the young Indian studio director who had just arrived panicked. The lack of training started to show. He told the anchors through the communication system to announce a break, but the system also malfunctioned at this time.

I was with the output team looking at the running order of the next bulletin. I ran to the PCR to ask the studio director to crash the bulletin and cut into a break.

Meanwhile Caroline and Mahreen bore the brunt of the technical failure and the clear lack of coordination between the PCR staff. After waiting for about a minute, Caroline walked to the PCR assuming that the studio director had taken her out of vision. She had worked for over 16 hours without a break for the last three weeks, and as she walked into the PCR she was in tears. She and her team had worked since early morning to put the half-hour show together.

There was a mad scramble in the server room and it was announced that the technical bug had been fixed and that we could resume the show. I held Caroline's hand and told her to go back to the studio to present the show. Anyone else in her position would have refused. She wiped her tears and went back in.

The technical glitches continued, and the programme schedules went awry. Each bulletin was delayed.

Atul came back from the launch ceremony and summoned me.

'The launch is trending on Twitter. They are talking about every mistake the team is making. Congratulations anyway for the launch,' he said, as an afterthought.

I was livid, but I had bigger issues at hand. It was appalling that he could talk to me this way. He had seen the team toiling against all odds, he knew the systems had not stabilised, he knew most of the equipment in the studio had been installed just a few hours ago – and he had the audacity to tell me about the mistakes?

The launch was the way it was because of his pig-headed

insistence on launching without a proper practice run with the full system operational. The launch was this way because he chose to arrogantly ignore DStv and not stick to the roll-out plan they had prescribed. The launch was this way because he decided to go ahead without training the staff.

The trickle of jokes on social media swelled into a tsunami by late night and had a crushing effect on the young team. They had to watch the fall-out of the wrong decision Atul had taken, against professional advice.

The systemic issues grew over the next few days. Despite the best efforts of the technical team, the systems continued to crash regularly. The play-out system, the communication connections, the graphic engines, the teleprompter – anything that could crash did. The newsroom automation system would malfunction, mostly because of user-related errors.

'Rajesh, there are some people on the team who are with the enemy and want to sabotage our venture. I know who they are, and I will punish them. The attack on social media is hurting me and my family. My children are the butt of jokes in their school. This must stop,' Atul told me two days after the launch.

I was amazed at how he thought the bugs in the system were sabotage. I have been part of many launches and know that it takes weeks for engineers from various system manufacturers to iron them out. Most networks fix the bugs during the dry or practice runs. There were no practice runs in this case. That too because of decisions taken by Atul himself. I had warned him of this before.

One afternoon shortly after lunch one of the bulletins was delayed by a couple of minutes because a play-out system crashed. I was in the PCR as the technical team was working in the server room to set the play-out right.

Atul stormed in and started taking pictures of the people in the room with his phone.

'You bloody monkeys. Fucking get out of here, pack your bags and go back to India. You are all useless people!' he screamed.

He then asked everyone in the PCR to stand up and introduce themselves.

'I know your names and have your pictures now. I know who the laggards are, and I will fire you and send you back home if there is one more mistake. All of you are useless pieces of shit,' he screamed.

This was not the first time Atul threatened and verbally abused the team. I confronted him about it. He said he did nothing wrong and would continue to berate anyone who he thought was 'screwing up'.

There was another incident the next day; this time Karun Shawney bore the brunt of his rage.

'Look down, you fool, how dare you look me in the eye when you talk to me. Don't you know I hate people who dare to look me in the eye? You bastards are fucking my channel and my reputation.'

Sound technician Warren Naidoo was at the receiving end of his rage one day when the audio system collapsed. Warren had worked until late the previous night and had to rush back to the office early the next morning as the sound technician on shift had called in sick.

He arrived 10 minutes after the shift started.

'You think this is a joke – you can come in anytime you feel like coming? I will throw out work shirkers like you right now. You think you can sabotage my TV station and get away with it? I know who is paying you people. I will sort you people out,' Atul shouted.

He tugged at Warren's hand as he screamed at him.

I had had enough. I would have failed as a leader if I continued to be part of management. My team was being abused for something they were not responsible for. All my life I had stood against abuse of this kind, and there was no way I would stand for it now. If I did not take drastic action, Atul would become more of a monster.

The threats to sack employees for what Atul perceived as mistakes, the shouting and screaming increased over the next few days.

I decided to hand in my resignation as soon as the systems showed improvement.

A few days later I sat down at my desk and began typing my resignation letter. I was full of anger and frustration. I wanted to write a long email detailing the reasons for my resignation.

But then I thought it would be futile. It could backfire because it would make Atul even more unreasonable and angry, and he would likely vent his frustrations on the staff.

I did not want a confrontation; I just wanted to exit this place as a mark of my protest against the illegal, unprofessional and unethical way in which the operations were being run by Atul.

I wrote a brief resignation letter that was polite in its tone. It did not seek to blame anyone or appear hostile in any way.

I mailed this to Atul, Laxmi and Nazeem.

When I look back at my last meeting with Atul and Laxmi, I realise that it would have been very difficult to change the corporate culture at ANN7. We were nothing more than paid servants and mouthpieces – servants who were coerced or co-opted into never questioning what was wrong and conditioned to turn a blind eye to the violations of the principles of journalism. We were servants who were expected to ignore the abuse and humiliation we were subjected to – because we were paid a salary at the end of the month.

I do sincerely hope ANN7 finds in its future editors the force that will break this mindset and unshackle the channel from the bonds that pin it down.

Epilogue

I LIVED IN SOUTH AFRICA for close to three months. During this time I experienced first-hand the intimacy that seems to exist between politics and crony business in the country.

This kind of crony capitalism is endemic in India and many other economies across the world. As a student of economics I have learnt that this intimacy drags growth, lowers government revenues and creates a wide chasm between the haves and the have-nots.

A mad scramble among the cronies to hoard licences and permits to plunder national resources, using innovative ways to illegally benefit politicians in power, has become accepted practice.

Billions of rands that should have gone to improving healthcare or education end up lining the pockets of greedy politicians and their cronies.

While this scourge is limited to the core sectors of the economy in many countries, its spread to the South African media, considered to be the fourth pillar of democracy, is a dangerous trend, to say the least.

I consider objectivity to be at the core of journalism.

I was unwittingly drafted in to be part of a sinister plan to build, in my opinion, a propaganda television channel. I quit because I did not want to be part of this. I quit because I did not want to compromise the values that have guided me for 20 years as a journalist.

I wrote this book to invite constant public scrutiny of this channel. I hope this vigilance will force the channel to be objective in the content it produces.

Acknowledgements

My wife Rashmi Sanyal has always been a pillar of strength. This book would never have been possible without her constant support and love.

Indentured: Behind the Scenes at Gupta TV was written at six different locations – Mumbai, Chennai, Delhi, Kathmandu, Pokhra and New Jersey. I would like to thank everyone who extended hospitality and warmth during my stay – Rahul Sundaram, my twin, and my sister-in-law Rajini, in Mumbai; Prakash Ezhumalai in Chennai; Rajneesh Bhandari and Chandrakant Jha while I was in Nepal; and Tejinder Singh in the United States.

I would like to thank my daughters Ananya and Ahana who make me so happy; my sister Susmita who always wishes the very best for me; and my nieces Geeta, Gayathri, Lakshmi and my nephew Vishnu who are so very loving.

A special thanks to my friends and colleagues of many years – Umesh Vohra and Shantanu Chatterjee – for being there for me.

A huge thanks to Bridget Impey for her faith in the book and supporting it despite immense political and legal challenges. Bridget, this book wouldn't have seen the light of the day without your steadfast belief. I would also like to thank Megan Mance, Nadia Goetham, Joey Kok and the entire team of Jacana Media for working on my manuscript and helping it become a book.

Index of names

The following is an index of the names of people who are mentioned in this book.

A
Aggarwal, Arun 32, 35, 36–7, 44–5, 49, 53–5, 62, 67, 69–71, 73, 89–91, 93–4, 96–9, 101, 117–8, 126, 136–7, 152
Aggarwal, Saurabh 39, 48–9, 149

B
Bhatia, Raman 33, 146
Blignaut, Charl 22–3, 26

C
Chatterjee, Shantanu 30, 32, 123, 125, 136–7, 141
Chawla, Ashu 33–4, 74, 94–101, 117–9, 125, 130–1
Chenia, Mahreen 123, 156–7
Coetzee, Margriet 7, 9–10, 13, 16–7, 45

D
Deepnarain, Sheena 106

E
Evans, Sarah 26

F
Frense, Amina 21–2

G
Gangat, Zaida 123
Garda, Imran 59
George, Jayosh 33, 36, 40, 44
Ghosh, Haranath 144–5
Goel, Jawahar 128
Goel, Laxmi 1–5, 7–12, 14–5, 17, 22–3, 25, 27–30, 32–4, 35, 37–40, 43, 44–5, 47–8, 50–2, 54–5, 57–8, 50–2, 54–5, 57–8, 62, 69–72, 73–9,

Indentured

81, 95–6, 109, 114–5, 124–8, 135–9, 141, 144, 147–8, 151–3, 156, 160
Gupta, Ajay 38–41, 55, 65–6, 68, 70–2, 73–5, 70–2, 73–5, 77, 83, 91, 93, 94, 97, 98–103, 118–21, 130–3, 136
Gupta, Atul 1–8, 10–3, 15–23, 25–6, 37–41, 43–4, 46–51, 53–4, 56–9, 61–3, 65, 67–72, 73–9, 82, 83, 84–8, 89–91, 93–4, 96–101, 103, 106–9, 111–5, 117–9, 124–5, 127–8, 129–30, 133, 135–40, 143, 144–9, 151–3, 156–60
Gupta, Tony 38–41, 55, 68, 70–1, 73, 88, 114, 137
Gupta, Virendra 12, 83–4

H
Howa, Nazeem 3, 5, 6–7, 17–23, 44–5, 47, 53–4, 56–7, 59, 61, 63, 68, 71, 73, 79, 85–6, 87, 93, 94, 99, 103, 106, 107, 108–9, 114, 118, 120–1, 125–7, 130, 133, 139, 140, 144–5, 151, 153, 160

K
Kamal, Aslam 3, 39, 48–9, 71, 89–90, 93, 94, 106, 145–6, 149, 151
Kanjirathingal, Roger Joseph 33, 36, 40, 44
Kohler, Quirin 24
Kumar, Sunil 128
Kumar, Suresh 24–5
Kumar, Uday 24, 32, 34, 35, 38, 40, 44, 71, 72, 95–6, 112, 149

L
Lachungpa, Kalden Ongmu 33
Laul, Revati 31
Lefafa, Tsunag 123
Leshoro, Benjamin 123

M
Mafokate, Arthur 143

Magwaza, Max 65–6
Mahomed, Nausheena 123
Makgoo, Ramaupi Arnold 123
Malema, Julius 129–30
Manyi, Jimmy 87–8, 108–9, 120
Mnisi, Lindokuhle 123

N
Naidoo, Warren 141, 159
Naidu, Mary 143, 152

O
Oosthuizen, André 110–1, 141

P
Pandey, Sanjay 14–8, 20, 24, 125, 135, 137, 148
Pandey, Varun 31
Patel, Imtiaz 68
Prasad, Krishna 36–8, 41, 43, 113
Puri, Ravi 128, 138–9, 142

R
Rantseli-Elsdon, Gerry 108, 130, 155
Rutiya, Siddharth 24, 35–8, 56, 62
Rutter Dros, Chantal 144–5, 155–6

S
Samuels, Caroline 123, 148, 156–7
Shankar, Vishnu 135–8, 148
Sharma, Dinesh 27–8
Sharma, Om 41
Shawney, Karun 31, 35, 38, 40–1, 43–4, 63, 159
Singh, Girish 51
Singh, Rahul 33, 56–7
Singh, Y P 29, 35, 38–41, 44, 47–9, 53–5, 61–2, 66–72, 73–9, 114, 124, 127–8, 138–9
Stemmet, Peter 123

T
Thomas, Laly 33–4
Tshabalala, Comfort 123

V
Vohra, Umesh 30, 32, 123–4, 141

W
Walshe, Nick 31, 58–9
Williams, Moegsien 20–2, 73, 77, 85, 86, 99, 103, 118, 130

Z
Zuma, Duduzane 95, 121, 131–3, 151, 153
Zuma, Jacob 5–6, 12, 46–7, 68, 82, 86–7, 90–1, 94–104, 108–9, 117–22, 129–33, 140, 151–2